What readers are saying al

Worth No Less is much more than an excellent read. It is a biblically sound approach to discovering God's invitation to live a life of purpose and eternal impact. As a pastor I've noticed that one of the greatest challenges to people's faith is not answering the question "Can God do this?" but rather, "Why would God choose me?" *Worth No Less* will help you see why God wants to use you. The real-life stories and Scripture found in these pages encourage us to see ourselves as God sees us, which leads to the faith needed to live the life God has called us to live.

~Jeremy Havlin, Senior Pastor of Renovation Church, Upstate SC

Everyone has a journey laced with difficulty, pain, and confusion. Jason found all of that in relation to the church and oftentimes the result of it. How God provided for him and kept him throughout the difficulties is a picture of the gracious and good God he serves. If you want some encouragement, hope, and even some smiles, this book is for you. You will be blessed and learn of the beauty and bounty found in Jesus.

~Will Lohnes, Senior Pastor of Hope Chapel, Greer, SC.

Worth No Less is an outstanding insight into the Father's love for every person, and how having an understanding of that love changes us from the inside out. I fully intend to use this great resource as a permanent fixture in our small group ministry, and after reading it, I'm sure you will feel the same way I do.

~Brad Lewis, Lead Pastor of The Edge Church, Greenville, SC

Honest emotions, real life struggles, and a foundation of God—that's what you'll find in *Worth No Less* from author Jason Thompson. He shares what happens when we open ourselves up to God, no matter the circumstances we face. This book points us back to the source of everything we need and reminds us of God's unfailing love. It's a book I'll cherish for myself and give as a gift again and again.

~Edie Melson, award-winning author & director of the Blue Ridge Mountains Christian Writers Conference

Jason writes with passion, authenticity and deep heart for discipleship. This book reads like he is sitting next to you in everyday conversation. Easy to read, theologically sound, and extremely challenging. A must read for those whose heart beats to make disciples.

~Jerry McCorkle, Director of Spread Truth Ministries

We know the Lord's plans are always good, but what level of "good" must we reach for Him to use us for His kingdom? In *Worth No Less*, Jason Thompson candidly shares his journey from worthless to priceless through the truth of God's Word.

~Vonda Skinner Skelton, Author, *Seeing Through the Lies: Unmasking the Myths Women Believe*

From its heart-filled introduction to the final pages, *Worth No Less* is an honest, healing exploration of our great value and purpose in the grace of Christ's Gospel. Thompson's transparent approach to sharing God's work in his life makes the hope of God's restoration and plan for our lives approachable, while still emphasizing the responsibility of ministry and depth of God's Word.

~Joshua J. Masters, Pastor, speaker, and author of *A Faith Unleashed: Living in the Hope of God's Rescue.*

WORTH
NO
LESS

Angie,

As a fellow follower of Christ, I
hope you will enjoy this book.
May God bless you and use you in
great and mighty ways!

Ephesians 3:20-21

WORTH NO LESS

Discover Your Value in Christ
and His Church

Jason Thompson

Stone Oak Publishing
A division of
Bold Vision Books
PO Box 2011
Friendswood, Texas 77549

Copyright © Jason Thompson 2021
ISBN 978-1-946708-65-6
Library of Congress Control Number 2021947590
All rights reserved.
Published by Stone Oak Publishing, a division of Bold Vision Books, PO Box 2011,
Friendswood, Texas 77549

Cover Design by Amber Wiegand-Buckley
Interior design by kae Creative Solutions
Published in the United States of America.

Unless otherwise indicated, all Scripture quotations are taken from the Holy
Bible, New Living Translation, copyright 1996, 2004, 2007, 2013 by Tyndale House
Foundation. Used by permission of Tyndale House Publishers, Inc., Carol Stream,
Illinois 60188. All rights reserved.

Scripture quotations marked (ESV) are from the ESV® Bible (The Holy Bible,
English Standard Version®), copyright © 2001 by Crossway, a publishing ministry
of Good News Publishers. Used by permission. All rights reserved.

Scripture quotations marked (NIV) are taken from the Holy Bible, New
International Version®, NIV®. Copyright © 1973, 1978, 1984, 2011 by Biblica,
Inc.™ Used by permission of Zondervan. All rights reserved worldwide. www.
zondervan.com. The "NIV" and "New International Version" are trademarks
registered in the United States Patent and Trademark Office by Biblica, Inc.™

》》》*DEDICATION*》》》》》》》》》》》》》》》》》

To my family - your love and support
made this book possible.

〉〉〉*TABLE OF CONTENTS* 〉〉〉〉〉〉

〉〉〉*FOREWORD* 〉〉〉〉〉〉〉〉〉〉〉〉〉〉〉

I am honored to write a foreword to this book by Jason Thompson. Jason documents, informs, and inspires you by giving you real insight into his spiritual growth and his calling. The best books show the struggles, sins, and successes of our walk with God. This book is written so powerfully, you literally weep when Jason weeps and rejoice when Jason rejoices. My ministry will utilize lessons from this book to help us be better disciples, and I believe both churches and individuals will benefit from this book.

~Dr. Phillip M. Baldwin
Pastor, Bethlehem Baptist Church

$\rangle\rangle\rangle$ *INTRODUCTION* $\rangle\rangle\rangle\rangle\rangle\rangle\rangle\rangle\rangle\rangle$

I could feel my heartbeat quicken and the tingle of cold sweat as I opened the report. I scanned the results and matched each grade to a specific student. I punched the numbers into my calculator, not quite able to believe what I was seeing.

***

Before becoming a pastor, I was an eighth grade English teacher. I worked at a Title I middle school, which is the designation given to a school which receives extra money from the government to counteract the effects of poverty. My school had the highest poverty percentage in the state at 93%. There was no good reason for our percentage being so high. We were positioned in a prosperous county, but our school zone looked like a jigsaw puzzle piece that conveniently avoided every affluent neighborhood nearby.

With many children from underprivileged homes, our test scores were typically terrible. We scored below average or unsatisfactory on most of the school's performance assessments. The state's solution was to throw money and meetings at the problem. Every student was given a laptop a full ten years before giving students a laptop became a thing. We had Smart Boards and Promethean Boards when other schools were still using chalk. We had low teacher/student ratios and a state assigned teaching specialist for every core subject. Highly decorated education gurus led us through professional development trainings.

Each year, we were given new toys, yet we continued to earn low test scores. Since we were receiving so much money and resources, there was a tremendous amount of pressure on our administration and faculty to prove we were doing everything in our power to help our students succeed. We documented and held meetings constantly. Stress levels went through the roof, which resulted in awful faculty retention numbers. In four years, I had three different principals, and more than half our teachers left for other schools or retirement. To give you an idea of how bad it was, in my second year of teaching, ever, I was given the English I Honors program because I was the longest tenured English teacher at the school.

The English I Honors program identifies high-achieving students and allows them to take a high school honors course while in eighth grade, providing a head start to their high school career. Adding this prep to my schedule more than doubled my workload. I taught five classes, and this one class consumed more than half of my time. So, when I found out the class only had ten kids, and that having only ten kids would make all my other classes bigger and harder to manage, I fought for some changes.

INVITATION TO STEP UP

I asked the principal, who was leaving for another district, if I could look over the test scores and add kids to my English I Honors class, who were close to making the cut. Since he already had one foot out the door and wouldn't be responsible for next year's results, the principal readily agreed and gave me the freedom to do whatever I thought best.

There were four designations for test scores—Advanced, Proficient, Basic, and Below Basic. We didn't have any students with Advanced test scores in English. The ones currently in the program scored Proficient on the test. I was proposing to add eight or nine of the Basic students to give myself a full class of honors students.

That's when I got greedy. It still bugged me that I was doing all this work for one class, one class out of five. I thought, *How awesome would it be to have two honors classes? If I invest in these kids and challenge them to work hard, I'm sure even more of them could handle an honors class.* So, I put all our Basic kids in the honors program. (We didn't have that many. Most of the grade level scored Below Basic on the test.) Once I added those kids, I was three or four short of a full class, so I looked over the test scores one more time and added a few more students, this time from the Below Basic ranks.

The next step was getting the parents to sign off on the class change. You couldn't just shove an unqualified student into an honors class without parents signing a permission form. Over the summer, I invited the unqualified students and their parents into a meeting where I told them I saw potential. I told them they were intelligent and fully capable of doing English I Honors work, and if they committed to the extra work of the honors program, they would be better prepared for high school.

Some parents openly expressed their shock. I remember one parent turning to her daughter and saying, "Girl, if you're so smart, why you coming home with Cs and Ds on your report card?"

"I don't know, mamma."

"Mr. Thompson, what makes you think my baby can handle this class?"

"I've seen her test scores. She's in the top twenty percent in her grade level. I see potential in her. She can do the work if she applies herself."

"Well, are you willing to do the work, girl?"

"Yes, mamma, I promise. Please let me take the class."

Most of my parent meetings followed suit. While I built up the abilities of these students, parents looked at their kids with a mixture of surprise and admiration, and the students beamed with pride and excitement. All but one parent signed off on the class change.

I would not have gotten away with this plan if we weren't between principals. I doubt I would have even tried if I knew how important English I Honors test scores were for a school performance report. I was just an inexperienced teacher who believed that all students could learn at a high level if you loved them, believed in them, and taught them well.

That's what I did that year. I poured my soul into my students. Those two honors classes stick out as two of my favorite classes of all time. We worked hard and played hard, and those kids made huge developmental leaps. I convinced them they were honors kids, and they owned that role. They took tremendous pride in telling others they were in Mr. Thompson's honors class.

GETTING THE RESULTS

At the end of the year, we began training for the big exam that would determine if they would receive high school credit for the class. This is when I learned two previously unknown details.

1. English I Honors test scores had a profound impact on a school's performance assessment.

2. Our school scored a 25% pass rating on last year's test.

Out of twelve students, students who actually qualified to take the test, only three had passed. Now three times as many students would take the test, over two-thirds who did not qualify for the class. I might have worried about incurring the wrath of our new principal if I hadn't already found out that our new principal was quitting at the end of the year.

As it was, I wasn't worried. I believed in my kids and was convinced we would shatter last year's 25%

pass rate. I doubted we would achieve the state's goal of 90%, but I was optimistic that we could reach at least 60% and maybe even as high as 80%. I spent those last few weeks before the test cramming, encouraging, and bribing. I told them I would buy everyone who passed their favorite candy bar, and we would throw a massive party if over half the class passed.

After my students took the test, we had to wait two weeks for the results. I tried to feel out my students on how they did, but I received a wide range of responses. Some bemoaned the amount of reading and admitted they didn't understand some questions, while others claimed they breezed through the test and wanted to know when we were going to have the party. Frankly, I wasn't sure which response worried me more.

I can still recall the moment when I realized the scores had been posted. I could feel my heartbeat quicken and the tingle of cold sweat as I opened the report. I scanned the results and matched each grade to a specific student. I punched the numbers into my calculator, not quite able to believe what I was seeing. 94% of my students passed the exam.

Trust me when I tell you that the party I threw those kids that Friday was epic.

THE GREAT TEACHER

Students thrive under teachers who believe in them and invest in them. The same principle applies to the church. And we have the best teacher possible in Jesus. Jesus perfectly demonstrated how to live. He provided a detailed textbook for us to follow. Then, He gift with 24-hour support through the Holy Spirit.

Jesus could not have invested in us more. He gave His life. He created us with unique gifts and abilities, and He perpetually calls us to partner with Him to create a Kingdom that will last forever. God knows exactly what we are capable of, both good and bad, and He chooses to build into us. We should ace every test with such a teacher.

Why are so many believers sitting on the sidelines? Why are so few Christians using their spiritual gifts for God's church? We aren't listening to the Teacher.

It is heartbreaking how few church attenders read the Bible regularly. I have been part of several life groups and men's Bible studies over the years. These groups usually take a break over the summer. Without exception, when we reconvene, at least half the group admits to not reading the Bible during the break.

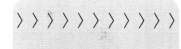

Why are so many believers sitting on the sidelines?

Prayer is a huge issue, too. I believe most Christians pray, but my pastoral experience has shown me that few prayer lives model Christ's. Maybe we offer a few words of thanks, but our brief prayers primarily include a list of requests often repeated night after night. Rare is the believer who asks *God* what He wants and then actually *listens.*

Then there's our learning environment. The church should be the one place everyone feels loved and valued. Where people encourage one another to use their gifts and grow in their faith and understanding. Whether the person who walks through those church doors is an unbeliever or a mature believer of sixty-plus years, the church should have a game plan for how to develop and plug them into God's Kingdom. That is what discipleship is all about.

Somewhere along the way, the church lost sight of its purpose. We stopped making disciples and became complacent in our comfortable existence. We failed to develop many of our spiritual gifts and built a reputation for being quick to tear down and slow to build up. Our words and actions contradict Jesus' teachings, and the result is most churches are filled with passive participants. We need to get back to being a church that trusts the life-changing power of God and invests in people.

PURPOSE

My hope is the Holy Spirit will use this book to open our eyes to the potential we have in Christ and His church. We are not meant to be bystanders. God has gifted each of us with unique gifts that are valuable to His church. The church will never be as strong and as healthy as it could be without each of us playing our part. God has great plans for us.

For we are God's masterpiece. He has created us anew in Christ Jesus, so we can do the good things he planned for us long ago (Ephesians 2:10).

If you think these words are too good to be true, I get it. I have been there before. I have felt unwanted. I have felt unqualified. I have questioned my worth. I will share my story and show you how God showed up in the lowest point in my life and called me to be a pastor. It makes little sense to me, but it's true. He took my sin and shame and turned them into tools for ministry.

Woven through the pages of this book, you will find other stories of redemption that reinforce this truth. No past is too messy for God to clean. No circumstance is too difficult for God to overcome.

This book is not a collection of stories, though. It is a Bible study that focuses on uncovering and dispelling the lies that prevent ministry work. At the heart of every hesitation to serve God is a lie. We believe lies about ourselves. We believe lies about God. And we believe lies about His church.

God's Word has answers for lies. We just have to crack open the book and study. There is no greater thrill for a teacher than to see students thrive in response to good teaching. The Great Teacher wants His students to graduate with honors. Let's embrace the truths found in His teaching and make God proud.

Chapter 1
Worthless?

I am fairly certain my grandparents never read a marriage book. They would have responded with blank stares if you asked them to identify their spouse's love language or quizzed them on "his needs" or "her needs."

My dad's parents frequently bickered and argued, and grandpa was well known for turning off his hearing aids once my grandmother got worked up.

On my mom's side, there is an often-shared story of how grandma chased grandpa around the house with a butcher's knife when she found out she was pregnant with my mom. She was not happy about getting pregnant in her 40s, and she had intentions of making sure it never happened again.

Despite their fights and frustrations, whether my grandparents would stay together was never in question. They took their vow "for better or for worse" seriously.

I never heard them say, "I love you," but we knew they loved each other deeply. They modeled steadfast devotion both in their marriage and in their faith. They left a godly legacy behind for their children, grandchildren, and great-grandchildren. A legacy I desperately hoped to live up to.

BROKEN VOWS

Both sets of my grandparents celebrated more than 60 years of marriage. My first marriage failed to make it to year six.

In 2007, shortly before my 29th birthday, I fell headlong into the abyss of divorce. The demise of my marriage hit me hard. When my wife no longer wanted to do life with me and wanted someone else instead, I was traumatized.

I could not stop crying. I woke up with tears. I showered with tears. I stained my pillows with tears.

Horrible thoughts and images, both real and imagined, bombarded my mind. I woke up night after night at 3:00 AM, wide awake and mind racing with a constant sense of dread.

I had missed three days of work in my first four years of teaching 8th grade English. I called in sick all five days during the first week of separation. It took a herculean effort to put on a fake smile and push through teaching the second week.

During each of my breaks, I closed and locked the door, buried my head in my arms, and sobbed. Five minutes before the bell rang, I pulled myself together, put a few eye drops in, unlocked the door and resumed the fake smile.

My grief gave way to full-on depression. I couldn't see past my pain and struggled to imagine a brighter future. I imagined ways to end my life without it looking like a suicide.

A friend convinced me to see a counselor who told me I was suffering from Post Traumatic Stress Disorder (PTSD). I always related the concept to soldiers or victims of violent crime. It seemed dramatic to label symptoms stemming from a broken relationship as PTSD, but the shoe fit too well for me not to wear it.

The counselor helped me realize that the source of my grief extended well beyond the loss of the marriage relationship. There was a much bigger factor stealing my hope and purpose. My divorce *stole my future and identity.*

LOSS OF IDENTITY

I was known as the good Christian kid who was immune to peer pressure. My reputation for resisting temptation was such that it became a competition among my friends, classmates, and coworkers to see which of them could convince me to smoke, drink, or have sex first. They all failed.

I took great pride in my reputation and worked hard to build upon it. I always went to church. I was a leader in my youth group. Shortly after graduating from a Christian college, I married a good Christian girl from a good Christian family. Then, I launched myself into teaching at a poverty-stricken middle school, openly sharing the Gospel with my students.

In my eyes, I had done just about everything right. So, how could a guy like me end up divorced? In my church world, divorce was a big sin, right below murder and just above fornication.

Sure, I had seen the statistics. Even the most conservative estimates show that more than a fourth of all Christian marriages end in divorce. But I assumed those numbers were skewed by all the people who claimed to be Christian but really weren't. In my mind, *real* Christians didn't get divorced.

Now, I was that disreputable guy who broke his vows. My sense of self-worth was based on a loving marriage and the respect of my peers. That shaky foundation was a pile of rubble now.

Have you ever lost your identity?

Maybe a secret sin came to light and changed everyone's perception of you. Perhaps you've lost a loved one, and life seemed to end. Or maybe you've experienced a career setback so severe that you've questioned your future and purpose.

Life experiences will hurt no matter who you are or how close you are to God. However, Christians should never feel utterly hopeless. Losing hope and purpose is a sign that something is wrong with our perception and our priorities.

Jesus is called the cornerstone in Scripture. He is the rock upon which we are to build. Paul warns us, "For no one can lay any foundation other than the one we already have—Jesus Christ" (1 Corinthians 3:11). Any attempt to build your life on a foundation other than Jesus is the equivalent of building a house on sand. The storms of life will wash away your foundation, and everything you built will come crashing down.

I had built my life on sinking sand, and now I was drowning. Completely devastated and overwhelmed, I clung to God.

CLINGING TO GOD

Like a non-swimmer gripping a life preserver while lost at sea, I white-knuckled my relationship with God. I prayed constantly. I read through the Bible in large chunks. I read every article and Christian book I could find. I sought advice from church leaders and counselors. I pursued each avenue I could think of in order to hear from God and feel His presence. And, He showed up.

God wrapped His loving arms around me and let me feel His presence.

Normally, I despise running if it doesn't involve chasing a ball or accomplishing some other sports-related purpose, but during this time, I ran. I prayed, and I ran.

My nightly runs felt like two-way conversations as healthy thoughts replaced negative ones and peace replaced angst.

"I'm not strong enough to get through this."

You don't have to be strong. I am enough.

"No one will ever love me again."

You are loved. You will feel loved again.

"What good is my life? I'm useless to You now."

I have a plan for you. Better than you can imagine.

QUESTIONING WHY

God's soothing words healed me, but it was a process. A process that I kept hijacking with questions. My personality type craves understanding and the ability to fit experiences in a nice little box. But my analytical brain could not make sense of my situation.

"Why did this happen?"

"How did this happen?"

"Why didn't my good choices protect me?"

"Why didn't my prayers for my marriage work?"

"What could I have done to prevent this?"

"What good could come from this?"

Have you ever bombarded God with questions? Maybe even screamed a few? Don't worry, God knows your pain, and He can handle your questions. Just don't expect immediate answers. God exists outside the constraints of time. A day is like a thousand years and a thousand years are like a day to Him. Rare is the occasion when our desired timeframe aligns with His will.

God responds to our questions when we are ready to receive the answer. The first answer I received to my questions was tough to hear. I wanted to know what I could have done differently, hoping the answer was "nothing". But God showed me I had a heart problem. My self-centered choices led to my brokenness. I may have been faithful and devoted to my marriage, but my devotion to God was superficial.

Keeping God at arm's length, I served Him in ways that were comfortable. I avoided "bad" actions and did "good" deeds out of pride and for the approval of others. In pursuing the validation of this world, I took back a large portion of the heart I had previously surrendered to God.

I thought I was living a pretty good life, but I was breaking the most important commandment. "You must love the Lord your God with all your heart, all your soul, and all your mind" (Matthew 22:37).

Half-hearted love for God led me down a path with more pain and emptiness than I could handle. I no longer wanted anything to do with that path. I was ready to be all-in for Jesus.

Unfortunately, while my heart was ready to serve God, Satan's many strongholds in my mind held me back. I believed my divorce made me

〉〉〉〉〉〉〉〉〉〉

Half-hearted love for God led me down a path with more pain and emptiness than I could handle.

worthless to God. I assumed people were ashamed of me, and no one would want to listen to what I had to say. I had never heard of a divorced elder or deacon, let alone a pastor. Even leading a small group seemed like a stretch for a disgraced divorcee like me.

Satan convinced me no godly girl would ever love me. And I had to choose between serving God or re-marrying and having children. The lies I believed about what God expected from me and for me crushed my spirit and left me resigned to second-class citizenship in His Kingdom.

I thank God for refusing to accept my resignation. He put godly men and women in my life that chipped away at the warped perception of my judgmental and legalistic frame of mind. This is why finding the right church is so important. Our spirits wither and die in toxic environments, and they thrive in healthy ones. We must connect to a life-giving church that replaces Satan's lies with God's truth and love. Finding the right church changed my life.

CHANGING CHURCHES

I grew up in a conservative, fundamental Bible church. A church where any kind of clapping or hand raising would earn dirty looks. Electric guitars and drums were of the devil. And wearing a pair of jeans to church was obscene. I attended this church for twenty years, from age 7 to age 27.

A burden to see my middle school students come to know Jesus motivated me to leave. I wanted to invite them to church, but their presence would have been a spectacle. Two entirely different worlds colliding—culturally, racially, and socioeconomically. Not to mention, they would have been bored out of their minds. It finally dawned on me that if I wasn't comfortable bringing my students to church, I was attending the wrong church.

A close friend introduced me to a small but growing nondenominational church. I wasn't entirely sure about the music and all the strange ways the church engaged people—repainting the walls to match every sermon series, creating hilarious football-related videos, and singing "Cheeseburger in Paradise" on an Easter Sunday, just to name a few. But the teaching was rich and inspired. Verses I had heard a thousand times came to life with the pastor's unique insights and life applications. The church embodied the most welcoming atmosphere I had ever experienced, inside or outside of church. Best of all—my students loved it.

The simple, unofficial service of picking up two or three students for church blossomed into a full-on bus ministry where I was packing up to 22 students in a 15-passenger van. (I know, not safe.) We were like a clown car pulling up to church as an unreasonable number of students piled out.

Busing kids to church was exhausting, but the experience filled me in a way that is difficult to explain. I felt like I was doing what I was supposed to be doing for the first time in a long time. My soul was coming alive at this church. My mind and my heart were growing, and my ministry involvement steadily increased.

In my past, I'd cringed at the thought of full-time ministry, equating the idea with being shipped off as a missionary to Africa or Asia. The thought of being a local pastor of any sort had never crossed my mind. Only the super religious went to seminary.

My new church had staff members who never attended seminary. They seemed like regular people with unimpressive backgrounds and experiences. I knew more about the Bible than most, but they were serving God on a level I had never dreamed of. God opened my eyes to the ministry potential I had—if I would say yes to God.

Two years into attending this new church, my heart burned for ministry work. I couldn't help thinking, *If only I hadn't lost my marriage. God could have used me in so many ways.*

ACCEPTING THE CALL

Shortly thereafter, my senior pastor asked me to lunch. After some brief small talk, he stopped me mid-bite with this statement:

"Jason, I want you to take over our College & Career class."

For a good five seconds, my mouth hung open in confusion and disbelief.

"What do you mean? I can't lead a class. My divorce isn't even final yet. You know that. What would people think?

"Everyone likes you. They respect you. No one is going to care that you're divorced."

"I'm pretty sure someone is going to care. Does the staff even know you're asking me?

"Yes, of course I talked it over with the staff, and they all agreed you are the right person for the job."

I had no intentions of saying yes, but the pastor was a convincing guy. We often joked that he could sell ice to Eskimos. I walked away from that meeting as the new College & Career leader, a role where I first realized my love for creating Bible studies.

A year later, my pastor asked me to breakfast. We were buttering our biscuits at Cracker Barrel when he dropped this bombshell on me:

"Jason, I want you to join our staff."

"What do you mean? Join your staff as what?"

"As a pastor."

"You can't be serious. Have you completely lost your mind? I can't be a pastor. I'm divorced!"

For me, the thought of becoming a pastor was ludicrous. All I could think about was what people would say when they found out I was divorced. I was sure they would either protest my hiring or dismiss anything I had to say. There was nothing my pastor could say or do to persuade me to take the job. I was convinced God would never want to use someone like me as a pastor.

A year later, he asked again.

"Really?" I responded. "You're serious about wanting me to join your staff?" I still thought he was crazy, but this time I at least tried to understand where he was coming from.

He pointed out my gifts and how they could be effective for ministry.

Ok.

Maybe.

He pointed out how many of our church members and volunteers came from broken homes, broken relationships, broken lives, "They will listen to you."

I remained unconvinced.

The role of pastor was sacred. No one else on staff had something as bad as a divorce on their resume. People expected more from a pastor.

Then, my pastor pulled the trump card. *God* told him to add me to his staff. A man I trusted and respected was telling me that God wanted me to be a pastor.

I thought about it and prayed about it ... a lot. Then, I told my pastor, "Maybe one day, but not now."

My heart was softening to the possibility, but I wasn't ready yet.

A funny thing happened the following year. Teaching English, something I planned to do my whole career, lost its flavor. Despite a supportive administration and wonderful students, I wasn't content. I could not shake the feeling that I wasn't where I was supposed to be.

When my pastor asked me to join his staff for a third time, I said, "Yes."

I left my comfortable, stable teaching job, took a huge pay cut, and joined a church staff with a frightfully uncertain future. It was one of the best decisions I have ever made.

I thought my past sin made me worthless. God showed me that my past made me worth NO less in His eyes.

The lie that held me back was thinking God wouldn't want to use someone who had been divorced. What lies are holding you back? What sin seems too heavy for God to redeem? What weaknesses have convinced you you're unqualified or unwanted? What fallacies have blinded you to your potential and purpose?

God called me to be a pastor. You don't have to be a pastor to play a significant role in God's Kingdom. Each part of the body of Christ has purpose and value. God gives spiritual gifts to His followers in order 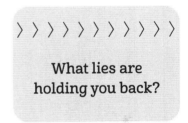 to fulfill a specific role in His Church, and the Church works better when we are all working together. Together, we can more effectively point people to Jesus.

What lies are holding you back?

I hope that through this journey we will recognize the lies holding us back, embrace the truth of the Gospel, and motivate one another to expect more out of ourselves, our church, and our relationship with God.

SMALL GROUP DISCUSSION QUESTIONS

1. What is your church background?

2. How have your experiences with church shaped your view of God, church, and ministry?

3. Have you ever felt worthless because of sin? If so, what do you think made you feel that way?

4. What would be your reaction if your senior pastor asked you to join the church's pastoral staff? Share your thoughts and feelings about such a prospect.

5. What character traits or habits would you need to build in order to be ready to take over a ministry at church?

Chapter 2
Lies

It took me a while to embrace the idea of being a pastor. For the first year or two, I refused to accept the pastor title. When others referred to me as "Pastor Jason," I'd jump in and say, "It's just Jason." If people asked what I did for the church, I said, "I'm the guy in charge of discipleship." When our leadership team forced us to get business cards, I chose the title "Discipleship Director." Even when our senior pastor became ill and I preached on Sunday mornings on a regular basis, I still cringed when people called me pastor.

Ten years into full-time ministry, I don't doubt God called me to be a pastor. I am filled with a burning desire to teach the Bible. My personal prayer and study time pointed me toward this full-time ministry position. Others, including the Elders of our church, have confirmed this calling and ordained me. The ministries I have been entrusted with have grown.

Why, then, was I so convinced God couldn't use someone like me? What made me feel so worthless and unqualified?

God didn't make me feel this way.

The enemy planted these thoughts in my mind. They were lies meant to minimize my effectiveness for God. Lies I swallowed while attending church.

SWALLOWING LIES

Churches should be sanctuaries of truth and love, but Satan has a knack for infiltrating our church bodies. Jesus refers to Satan as the "father of lies" (John 8:44). This liar delights in destroying God's people.

> *Stay alert! Watch out for your great enemy,*
> *the devil. He prowls around like a roaring lion,*
> *looking for someone to devour (1 Peter 5:8).*

Our great enemy is also a thief. He tries to steal our peace, our joy, and our contentment. Jesus warns us in John 10:10, "The thief's purpose is to steal and kill and destroy."

But here's the thing, Satan cannot directly harm or forcibly destroy God's church. God is infinitely more powerful than Satan, and our enemy has no power over us unless we give it to him. But that's what we do. We give it to him.

Every lie we believe about God allows Satan to build a stronghold in our heart—a place where he warps our perceptions. The more strongholds Satan has, and the longer they remain, the easier for him to convince us to sin. It is sin which leads to pain and suffering.

Essentially, Satan must convince us to pursue a path of self-destruction rather than a path of righteousness, and he's doing an incredible job of it. People are suffering mentally, emotionally, physically, and spiritually.

All of this pain started with a lie and is fueled by lies. And our churches are not immune. We have consumed an endless stream of lies, deceptions, and false teachings. It would be impossible to list, let alone provide commentary on every lie consumed by believers. So, I am going to focus on one big lie in this book— the lie that God doesn't want to use you to accomplish great things in His Kingdom.

Variations of this lie include statements such as:

"My past is too messy."

"I've screwed up too many times."

"I'm not good enough."

"I don't have the right gifts."

"I don't know enough."

"I'm too young."

"I'm too old."

This list could go on and on. All these lies serve the same purpose, to prevent the children of God from serving the Kingdom of God. These lies live and breathe within the church. At times, they are explicitly communicated from the pulpit due to a warped view of Scripture. Even more often, lies are implied by the choices, attitudes, and off-handed comments of various members of the church.

WEIGHED DOWN BY BAGGAGE

I am unnerved by the number of lies I allowed to take root in my heart. Each one created a stronghold that blinded me to truth and healing.

1. I believed that my good deeds were enough to earn God's favor. This lie prevented me from a deeper, personal relationship with Him. I read the Bible, but talking to God was awkward and forced. Listening for the Holy Spirit's voice never crossed my mind.

2. I thought my strict code of conduct would protect me from harm. This lie made my divorce even more devastating. I assumed God was punishing me, and I didn't understand why. I felt powerless and unprotected.

3. I believed that major mistakes forever relegated God's children to second-class citizenship. This big lie crushed my spirit and blinded me to my purpose. I am a pastor today because I had mentors who stubbornly pursued me and showered me with truth.

Ultimately, the baggage we collect is our choice. Only when we hold on to Jesus and His Word can we recognize and reject the lies around us. We do ourselves a disservice when we ignore the influence our circumstances and environment have on our perspective. The church I grew up in played a huge role in shaping the faulty perspectives that weighed me down. I believe it shared the same positives and negatives found in the church of Ephesus described in Revelation 2. The church was excellent at not tolerating evil people and fighting false teaching, but it was lacking in love. The fear of God was in ample supply there, but displays of love and affection were hard to find.

I plugged into the church through high school and college. But, after college, there was simply nothing for me. Deacons and Elders were older, highly respected, usually well-off businessmen that were voted in by the congregation. Most of our Sunday school teachers were professors from the local Christian university, with doctorates on their resume. It may have been my perception, but I felt there were no significant opportunities available to me. Certainly, no one was inviting me to do more or be more for Christ and His Church.

> > > > > > > > > > >

The church is failing to motivate believers to do more and be more.

I don't think my experience is unique. I believe the vast majority of churchgoers feel unqualified and uninvited. I believe most churches in America have a fuzzy view of discipleship and few genuine growth opportunities. The church is failing to motivate believers to do more and be more.

The primary purpose of the church is found in Hebrews 10:24-25, "Let us think of ways to motivate one another to acts of love and good works. And let us not neglect our meeting together, as some people do, but encourage one another, especially now that the day of his return is drawing near." Encouraging each other is why we meet together as we motivate one another to love more, serve more, and connect more to Christ and His body.

MAKING AND EQUIPPING DISCIPLES

Before ascending to heaven, Jesus told his disciples to make disciples (Matthew 28). Not to save people (only God can do that). Not to increase Sunday morning attendance. Not to tell people what they could or could not do for God. We are to make disciples. We are to welcome people in, invite them to a more fulfilling life through Christ, model for them what following Christ looks like, and equip them to follow Christ and serve His Kingdom.

Ephesians tells us that Christ gave five gifts to the church—the apostles, the prophets, the evangelists, the pastors, and the teachers. The purpose of these gifts is made abundantly clear in Ephesians 4:12-13.

Their responsibility is to equip God's people to do his work and build up the church, the body of Christ. This will continue until we all come to such unity in our faith and knowledge of God's Son that we will be mature in the

Lord, measuring up to the full and complete standard of Christ.

These five groups of people are supposed to equip God's people, the Church, the body of Christ. Every person who has accepted Christ and joined the body of Christ is to be discipled and equipped. And we don't stop equipping everyone until they meet the full and complete standards of Jesus. Do you know anyone who has attained Jesus' level of perfection? Yeah, me neither. Growing and equipping people is a job that isn't supposed to stop on this side of heaven.

Why are so few church leaders inviting and challenging people to be fully equipped followers of Christ? Why are so many people content with attending church and doing little else?

DANGERS OF FALSE TEACHING

The father of lies is effective. He sows lies and promotes liars. The parable of the wheat and weeds found in Matthew 13 illustrates this truth. While the farmer (God) actively sows his field with wheat (believers/ the truth), an enemy (Satan) slips in at night and sows weeds (false believers/lies).

The Bible frequently warns us against false teaching. Peter provides us with a prime example in 2 Peter 2:1-3 when he states, "But there were also false prophets in Israel, just as there will be false teachers among you. They will cleverly teach destructive heresies and even deny the Master who bought them. In this way, they will bring sudden destruction on themselves. Many will follow their evil teaching and shameful immorality. And because of these teachers, the way of truth will be slandered. In their greed, they will make up clever lies to get hold of your money. But God condemned them long ago, and their destruction will not be delayed."

Peter warns us that false teachers will try to twist the Gospel, convince us that Jesus isn't the only way to salvation, deny that certain sins are sins, make the truth sound scandalous, and get hold of your money.

Yep, that sounds about right.

Satan rarely uses big, obvious lies to deceive us; rather, he uses small deviations from the truth to knock us slightly off course. Imagine walking along a straight path that pointed due North. If you were to turn one degree to the right, you wouldn't leave that path right away. Take ten steps, and you're probably still on the path. Walk ten miles, and it would probably take a pair of binoculars to see where you're supposed to be. Walk 10,000 miles, and you're probably not even on the same continent. Many churches and individuals within the body of Christ have been walking slightly off course for a long, long time. The lies we believe keep us shackled to sin, shame, complacency, and hypocrisy.

MISAPPLIED SCRIPTURE

The cure for deception is a healthy dose of truth. It is also helpful to pull up the root causes of the lie. So, before we inspect the truth of the Gospel, let's look at a few specific misuses of Scripture that have played a role in making believers feel unqualified.

1 Corinthians 5 is one of the passages Satan twists to influence Christians to be judgmental. In this chapter, Paul blasts the Corinthians for allowing a church member to have an ongoing sexual relationship with his stepmother. No doubt, this was a legitimate issue that needed correction. Paul recommends kicking the man out of the church until he repents.

Verse 11 is the one often taken out of context: "But now I am writing to you that you must not associate with anyone who claims to be a brother or sister but is sexually immoral or greedy, an idolater or slanderer, a drunkard or swindler. Do not even eat with such people" (NIV).

Churches have taken this verse and created a theology where righteousness equates with avoiding sinners. When sin is revealed, care and affection are replaced with moral outrage. This mentality could not be further from the heart of God.

First of all, we are all sinners. We should be careful not to view our sins as more palatable to God than the sins listed in this passage. The church has been busy judging the world when Paul never intended it to. The verses surrounding verse 11 make Paul's intention clear.

But I wasn't talking about unbelievers who indulge in sexual sin, or are greedy, or cheat

*people, or worship idols. You would have to
leave this world to avoid people like that ... It
isn't my responsibility to judge outsiders, but it
certainly is your responsibility to judge those
inside the church who are sinning. God will
judge those on the outside*
(1 Corinthians 5:10,12-13).

Judging people outside the church is off the table. What about sinners inside the church? Can we at least judge them? Well, that depends. Have the guidelines in Matthew 18 been met?

Jesus provides us with a blueprint for handling sin in the church. First, one person is supposed to confront a fellow believer, *privately.* If the person repents, that's the end. If not, then two or three believers should gather together and confront the offender. If he or she still refuses to repent, church leadership is to be brought in. Only when a believer rejects the church's counsel to repent is church discipline to be used.

Imagine a church that followed this teaching. As soon as sin was seen, it was corrected. Those who refused to repent were asked to leave. Our churches would be so much healthier.

Instead, we skip the loving confrontation part and head straight for the judging condescension. While giving dirty looks, spreading gossip and avoiding noticeable sinners comes naturally for many Christians, we cringe at the thought of encouraging a believer to stop sinning one-on-one.

Even worse, we don't limit our judgment to unrepentant sin, as the Bible commands. Paul didn't hate the man who was sleeping with his stepmom. Love motivated his recommendation to cut ties with this man. Paul loved the church enough to protect it from being tainted by sin, and he loved the man enough to motivate him through harsh discipline. The goal was repentance, not punishment.

I believe Paul is referencing the same man in 2 Corinthians 2:5-8.

I am not overstating it when I say that the man who caused all the trouble hurt all of you more than he hurt me. Most of you opposed him, and that was punishment enough. Now, however, it is time to forgive and comfort him. Otherwise he may be overcome by discouragement. So I urge you now to reaffirm your love for him.

Paul encouraged the church to forgive and comfort those who repent. Repentant sinners should feel our love and acceptance. Our hope and prayer should be full restoration. The Bible does not suggest a glass ceiling for people being restored because there is no limit to Christ's power to re-

> 〉 〉 〉 〉 〉 〉 〉 〉 〉 〉
> **Our hope and prayer should be full restoration.**

store, redeem, and renew. Walls and barriers in our pursuit of Christ are self-imposed walls founded on false teaching.

Our tendency to push our values on outsiders and hold past sins over the heads of insiders has created a culture problem. Those with a criminal history, or a drug addiction, or homosexual tendencies feel unwelcome in our churches. Church members who struggle with marriage problems, rebellious children, or insurmountable debt are shamed into silence, afraid to reveal their issues. Meanwhile, church members displaying pride, anger, gossip, gluttony, or materialism get a pass.

Our church culture is completely backwards. We shouldn't concern ourselves with the world's sins. Believers who have overcome past sin should be celebrated rather than shamed. They should be plugged in rather than disconnected. Our focus should be on correcting the unrepentant sins we've given a pass to for so many years.

I can think of countless examples of how these cultural issues have damaged the church's reputation. One that comes to mind happened a number of years ago in my town. An aspiring businessman bought a building across the street from a local church. He invested his savings planning to turn it into a convenience store. When church members realized his intention, they mobilized. They didn't want a convenience store so close to their church. Those kinds of places sold alcohol and attracted all kinds of riffraff. Something had to be done.

Church members wrote editorials to the local newspaper voicing their outrage. Church leaders took them to court in an attempt to block the store's liquor license. The store complied with city ordinances banning alcohol sales within 300 feet of a church, but it violated the county ordinances requiring a 500-foot buffer. The store was right on the city line. It could go either way.

The businessman was devastated. He knew his store would not survive without liquor sales. He pointed out the two grocery stores already selling alcohol within 500 feet of the church. One faced the front of the church, and the other was situated directly behind his convenience store. How could his liquor license be a problem?

As the court battle dragged on, the inevitable happened. The man's store failed to make money, and he had to sell the property, losing much of his investment in the process.

While this battle played out, unknown to anyone outside of church leadership, a youth leader was revealed to be a pedophile. This news did not make the papers. No parent was ever told. No child ever received counseling or an apology. The man was removed from serving with children, but that was it. The revelation was swept under the rug where the church could pretend it didn't happen.

These events are not unique to my town. Communities all over the nation could share similar experiences. Churches voice outrage over issues they are not called to speak into, while hiding flaws that should be exposed for the sake of healing. As a result, we've built a reputation for being judgmental hypocrites.

JUDGMENTAL AND HYPOCRITICAL

A study conducted in the late 2000s by LifeWay Research reported that 72% of those who don't attend church were reluctant because they believe the church was "full of hypocrites." The Barna Group conducted a study focusing on the perception of youth (ages 16-29) and found that a whopping 87% of those who don't attend church see Christianity as judgmental and 85% saw it as hypocritical.

Judging others wins no one to Christ. Our love for one another does. Outsiders should want what we have. Our peace and joy should draw them in. The church is Christ's chosen instrument for sharing the Gospel and initiating spiritual healing. There is no plan B. Our churches have to become more Christ-like.

We can't change the past. All we can do is chip away at these negative perceptions with our love and service. We cannot hide, ignore, twist, or water down the truth. That's not love. Telling people what they want to hear is self-centered and destructive. Love and truth go hand in hand. But, for every hard truth we have to share, we should lavish on a hundred loving words of encouragement and acts of service.

As Peter wisely instructs in 1 Peter 3:15-16, "And if someone asks about your Christian hope, always be ready to explain it. But do this in a gentle and respectful way. Keep your conscience clear. Then if people speak against you, they will be ashamed when they see what a good life you live because you belong to Christ."

Be gentle and respectful. We must live such good and loving lives that people who know us will be ashamed to bash us. Earning this kind of reputation will require work. We need God to fill us, and we need the whole body of Christ working at full capacity to turn this ship around and change the church's reputation.

INTIMIDATING STANDARDS

1 Timothy 3 and Titus 1 offer helpful leadership guidelines. Unfortunately, these passages are often used to deter believers from embracing the ministry call of God. 1 Timothy 3 is intimidating. It's specific, yet it leaves a lot of room for interpretation. Historically, some qualifications have been rigorously adhered to, while others have been largely ignored.

The passage starts with "So an elder must be a man whose life is above reproach." Well, that's kind of daunting. What exactly is the standard of "above reproach"? Does that mean that *no one* has *anything* bad to say about the guy? Or is the standard not quite that lofty?

Then there's this: "He must be the husband of one wife." These words are where the fighting begins. Some argue that divorcees are disqualified from eldership—reasoning that a person can't have more than one wife and those who divorce and remarry have had multiple wives. But the passage isn't using any form of past tense. The man in consideration must *be* the husband of one wife. Currently, he must have only one wife. Polygamy was fairly common during this time period, and Paul rightly considered polygamy to be an unhealthy and problematic practice for an elder.

I do not believe this line excludes a man who had been divorced any more than it excludes widowers who remarried or bachelors who never married. Yes, it says an elder must be the husband of one wife, but that would exclude Paul himself from being an elder, so it seems clear Paul was addressing the problem of polygamy.

"He must exercise self-control, live wisely, and have a good reputation." Those are broad, reasonable strokes eliciting little debate. Those characteristics are difficult to define, but they are easy to recognize when present.

"He must enjoy having guests in his home ... " My wife is an extreme introvert, and while I have some social extrovert tendencies, I am naturally wired as an introvert, too. Neither of us has the gift of hospitality. Hosting people is exhausting for us, and we don't do it nearly as often as we should. Should that disqualify me?

OVERLOOKED QUALIFICATIONS

The qualifications for an elder finish this way.

"He must not be a heavy drinker or be violent. He must be gentle, not quarrelsome, and not love money. He must manage his own family well, having children who respect and obey him. For if a man cannot manage his own household, how can he take care of God's church.

"An Elder must not be a new believer, because he might become proud, and the devil would cause him to fall. Also, people outside the church must speak well of him so that he will not be disgraced and fall into the devil's trap."

That's a lot to break down. Not being violent or prone to drunkenness are no-brainers. It's a shame that some pastors and elders display these qualities, but it's an even bigger shame that Christians feel unqualified and unwelcome to ministry opportunities because they have displayed these characteristics in the *past*. Again, this list is referring to the qualities that currently describe a candidate, not distant offenses.

An elder should be gentle, not quarrelsome, and not love money. These qualities are rarely emphasized and often overlooked in our pastors and elders. Gentle is not a word that comes to mind when I think of senior pastors, and for a group that is not supposed to be quarrelsome, there is a lot of bickering and arguing amongst church leaders. The whole love of money aspect among senior leadership is a black hole that we could get sucked into for chapters on end. A number of high-profile church leaders have been forced out of ministry over these qualifications. Unfortunately, it usually takes years of verbal and emotional abuse before a church ousts a pastor, and it usually takes years of shady financial decisions before their greed comes to light. We usually ignore these characteristics until it is far too late.

An elder must also manage his house well, complete with obedient, God-fearing children. Yikes. Unfortunately, "pastor's kids" are often known for being entitled brats. Many go through a season of wild rebelliousness. I have often wondered if preacher kids go wild because the family is under greater spiritual attack or whether the kids naturally rebel against the pressure to be perfect. Perhaps the bigger issue is the struggle to maintain a healthy balance between ministry work and family time. It's hard to say for sure why it happens, but family problems are common in ministry. But it's rare for pastors to step down over them. Meanwhile, the pain and embarrassment of family dysfunction keeps a lot of talented and godly people on the sidelines, unaware God can use them too.

THE THIN LINE BETWEEN MINISTRY AND INACTIVITY

An elder shouldn't be a new believer. I wonder what kind of timeframe Paul had in mind. The book of Acts says Paul preached about Jesus in the synagogues a few days after his conversion (Acts 9:20). Galatians seems to indicate that he spent three years in Arabia being prepared for ministry by Christ himself before he presented himself to the apostles and was officially sent out. I like a three-year plan. Jesus' public ministry with the 12 disciples was three years.

With our glacially slow modern-day discipleship process, a new believer might need a decade or two before they feel capable, knowledgeable, and qualified enough for leadership.

We cannot afford to move so slowly or turn so many people away. My purpose in discussing these biblical passages is to point out that most pastors fail various parts of this qualification list, and most believers are too intimidated to even throw their hat in the ring. For far too long, Satan has convinced churches to use the passages in Timothy and Titus to disqualify those God has called into ministry. Churches should get out of God's way and start helping Him disciple everyone, as we've been called to do. We have to invite and challenge believers to do more for Christ and embrace more significant roles in His Church. We need to stop imagining a huge chasm between ministry leaders and laypeople. The gap is a thin line. On one side are those who have said yes to the calling on their lives. On the other side are those who have said no, or aren't even aware they've been called.

God wants to use each of us in a powerful way. It's a lie that you can't attain the qualities that best describe the most godly men and women in the church. It's a lie that you can never own a reputation that is beyond reproach. Nothing is impossible with God. He can accomplish anything through us when we say yes to Him.

Let's stop believing the lies and focus on the truth.

SMALL GROUP DISCUSSION QUESTIONS

1. How would you explain the church's tendency to have such a high percentage of members who are not plugged into serving or leading?

2. What do you think are some damaging lies churches have embraced over the years?

3. Satan loves to use scripture for his own purposes. Can you think of any passages that have been twisted for his purposes? If so, share an example with the group.

4. What lies have you had to overcome in your personal walk with Christ?

5. How can we counteract the effects of the lies that are planted in our minds and in our churches?

Chapter 3
Truth

I was a voracious reader growing up. I won a 2nd grade reading contest by reading 116 books in a week. My love affair with literature continued into adulthood and served as my primary motivation for teaching English. I love all types of literature, but I am a sucker for a good fantasy series. Two of my favorites are *The Chronicles of Narnia* and the *Harry Potter* series. These two series are incredible for many reasons, but I love how they portray the difference between magic motivated by love and magic motivated by self-interest. The heroes are motivated by love, loyalty, friendship, and justice. The villains are motivated by anger, hate, power, and pride. The heroes give up their lives to save lives, and they are restored to life. The villains take lives to control lives, and their lives end in death.

These stories mimic the greatest story ever told, the story of the Gospel.

ALL ABOUT JESUS

The Gospel story begins and ends with Jesus. It is all about Him and all for Him. To tell it best, I think we should start at the beginning.

In the beginning was the Word, and the Word was with God, and the Word was God. He was in the beginning with God. All things were made through him, and without him was not any thing made that was made. In him was life, and the life was the light of men. The light shines in the darkness, and the darkness has not overcome it (John 1:1-5 ESV).

The rest of John 1 makes it clear the Word is Jesus. In the beginning, Jesus already existed. He has always existed with God, and it is through Jesus that everything was made.

This is confirmed in Colossians 1:16, "For by him all things were created, in heaven and on earth, visible and invisible, whether thrones or dominions or rulers or authorities—all things were created through him and for him" (ESV).

He is the source of life for mankind. So, when we read the creation account in Genesis where it tells us, "In the beginning God created the heavens and the earth," the Trinity (God the Father, God the Son, and God the Holy Spirit) works together to bring about the creation of the universe. That is why we see the plural form used in the creation narrative. Genesis 1:26 states, "Then God said, 'Let *us* make human beings in *our* image, to be like *us*'" (emphasis mine).

Many Bible scholars teach physical encounters between God and man in the Old Testament are with Jesus in his preincarnate form. (Some examples include God's direct interaction with Adam and Eve, Abraham, Moses, and Gideon.)

When I read Genesis 2, I picture Jesus taking dirt and forming it into the shape of a man and breathing the breath of life into his nostrils. I picture Jesus laying Adam down in a deep sleep to remove a rib from his side and fashion that rib into the beautiful form of a woman.

THE REASON FOR SUFFERING

The creation story has a beautiful beginning. But, like all great stories, there must be some drama if we are to experience the exhilaration of redemption. And we find some serious drama in Genesis 3. Adam and Eve make a mess of their paradise world with their rebellious fruit choices. Their sin paves the way for pain, suffering, and death to invade creation.

Perhaps the most frequent and most difficult question skeptics ask about God is "If God is good, and loves us, why is there so much pain and suffering in the world?" It's a valid question with no easy answer, and we'll never be able to fully explain it on this side of heaven. But a couple of truths from scripture help us.

Pain and suffering were not God's intended purpose for His children. That's not how He created us, and that's not how the story will end. God created a paradise world without sin, without pain and suffering, and one day He will recreate the heavens and the earth and make them perfect. He will wipe away every tear, and there will be no more sin, no more death, and no more suffering. (Revelation 21:1-4)

God did not create sin. He does not want His creation to suffer. His intentions for us are good and righteous. But why did God allow sin into the world, knowing the consequences of sin are always pain and suffering?

LOVE IS THE REASON

To understand why God allowed sin, we need to understand why He created us. I have completely forgotten the catechisms that were drilled into me as a young boy, with one exception.

Q: "What is the chief end of man?"

A: "To glorify God and enjoy him forever."

I think this catechism stuck in my mind because it resonated with me as the purpose of life. We exist to bring God glory and to enjoy a loving relationship with Him, forever. That is our purpose.

John said, "God is love" (1 John 4:16b). Love is His very nature, and God created us to extend His love. He created us in order to pour out His love on us and receive love from us in return, and in this love, He receives the glory He rightly deserves.

God's purpose for creating us is mirrored by parents who want children. Why do parents choose to invest their time, energy, and love into their children? Because they hope their children will share their love and become a lifelong source of pride and joy. No one would plan a pregnancy if they knew their child would grow up hating and rejecting them, while being a constant source of shame. The hope is love, pride, and joy. Sometimes the reality is hate, shame, and pain. If you want to experience love, you have to risk rejection.

Love is a choice. It is often coupled with strong feelings and emotions, but love is intertwined with our ability to choose, and it is affected by our thoughts and actions. We can think and act in ways that will increase our love, or we can think and act in ways that decrease our love. Love can come naturally, or it can be labored. We can be cruel to someone we love, and we can be kind to someone we don't love, but what is in our heart is revealed, eventually.

The ancient Greeks had six words for love, and it still wasn't enough to explain what we humans mean by love. Love is impossible to define, but this much is clear. You cannot force love. You can force someone to say or do something, but you cannot force someone to love you.

No one knows this better than God, whose very nature is love. The only way He could create an extension of His love and receive true love in return is to create us with the free will to choose. God risked the inevitable rejection of men and women in order to experience the pride and joy of having His children love Him.

If God removed our free will and forced us to obey and say we loved Him, we would be nothing more than glorified robots or puppets on a string. When I've explained this concept in our church's beliefs class, I brought a doll—one of those dolls that say phrases when you push a button. If you push the button where the heart is located, the doll says, "I love you." This doll is a pretty neat feature for a child. They light up at hearing the various phrases, at least initially. But even a child gets bored with such a doll before long. But how much pleasure does an adult get from such a toy? Would a mother light up when she heard "I love you" after pushing the button? Of course not. No adult would confuse that action for love.

Now, picture this. You arrive home after a long day at work. The moment you open the door to your house, your child stops what he or she is doing and runs across the room, jumps into your arms and says, "I love you mommy" or "I love you daddy."

There's simply no comparison. God, who is infinitely greater and more deserving of love is determined to claim as His own a vast number of sons and daughters who truly love Him and honor Him, even though He knows there will be an even greater number who reject Him and go their own way.

PARADISE LOST AND FOUND

Yes, God knew we would mess up His creation. He knew if He gave mankind free will, sin would enter the world and a great number of people would reject Him. In His infinite wisdom and understanding, He decided that a world with free will, love, and redemption in it was better than a world without it.

It wasn't like God dealt Adam and Eve a tough hand, either. He stacked the deck in their favor. Adam and Eve lived in a paradise world. Everything was easy for them. They only had one rule. They could do whatever they wanted except eat the fruit of one tree, the Tree of the Knowledge of Good and Evil. Their minds weren't capable of coming up with other sinful actions. They were innocent and pure, able to enjoy every experience and pleasure God gave them—as long as they obeyed God's one command.

Many have wondered why God bothered to give them this one command. Why not allow everything? Once again, the reason is love. Another key attribute of love and devotion is sacrifice. The best love involves a selfless giving of oneself, a willingness to care for someone even when it doesn't benefit you. God had given them everything they had. Giving back to God something that He had given them was the only way they could show God sacrificial love and devotion. This concept still applies. Every good thing we have or experience comes from God, and the only way we can show our love and devotion is to give Him back a portion of what He's given us. Unfortunately, we have a hard time seeing our talents, resources, and money as His.

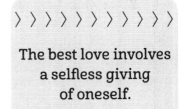

The best love involves a selfless giving of oneself.

God asked Adam and Eve to give back one tree out of a world full of trees. We all know what happened next.

Satan entered the serpent. The serpent tricked Eve. Eve ate the fruit and gave it to Adam. Adam ate the fruit, and they felt shame over their naked bodies. Paradise lost.

Each physical encounter between God and mankind is Jesus revealing Himself in one form or another. So, when Genesis 3:8 tells us that God came to the Garden of Eden for His evening stroll with Adam and Eve, I picture Jesus calling out "Where are you?" "Who told you that you were naked?" After a lot of finger-pointing, Jesus explains the consequences of their actions and details the resulting curse on men, women, and nature.

The most significant detail of the curses handed out involves the curse spoken over the serpent. In Genesis 3:15, God tells the serpent, "And I will cause hostility between you and the woman, and between your offspring and her offspring. He will strike your head, and you will strike his heel."

Over the centuries, there has been a lot of animosity between women and snakes. Most women (not to mention a fair share of men) I know are deathly afraid of them, and there's no better example than my mother. My mother is a saint. She is one of the kindest, most thoughtful and wonderful people you could hope to meet. But, if she finds out that someone owns a snake, she immediately writes off that person as either crazy or evil or both. One of my younger brothers once made the mistake of telling my mom he saw a snake in our basement. She refused to enter the basement or let anyone up through the basement door for two weeks. Four of us kids roomed in the basement. We had to exit our house through a basement door, climb our back steps, and reenter the house through the back door. Since she refused to enter the basement where she usually did our laundry, we made my younger brother do the family laundry for two weeks as punishment for opening his big mouth. When it comes to snakes, mamma don't play.

People dislike snakes and want to get rid of them. To do so, you typically attack its head. Hitting or grabbing it anywhere else will just allow the snake to bite you. If you come across a snake without realizing it, and it attacks first, it's likely to get you on the heel or ankle. God's curse became a reality, but so much more is going on here.

On a deeper level, this serpent also represents Satan. God promises that Eve's offspring, one of her descendants, would destroy Satan. This is the first messianic promise found in Scripture. It's a promise from the Son of God about the Son of God. One day the Son of God would be born of a woman. Satan would attack His heel (which is fulfilled when nails were driven through His feet), and Jesus would destroy Satan. Satan may still run around, but he's already had his favorite weapons, sin and death, taken away. He's on borrowed time, and his ultimate demise is assured.

Before He created the world, God knew the plan He would use to redeem mankind from its sin, providing a way for men and women to maintain a loving relationship with their Creator—despite sin. God was not caught by surprise. He did not have to scramble to come up with a solution. His plan was always to send His one and only Son to earth to model what a loving relationship with our heavenly Father should look like. He would die for us to make atonement for all of our sins. Through Jesus' sacrifice, our destiny shifted from death to life, from eternal separation to eternal love.

The purpose of the Old Testament is to point forward to Jesus. The purpose of the New Testament is to point back to Jesus' life, death, and resurrection. It is all about Him and all for Him.

THE CONSEQUENCES OF SIN

Now that we've established the broad backdrop of the Gospel, let's look at some specific New Testament passages that help explain why Jesus had to die and how His death and resurrection lead to eternal life and love.

> *When Adam sinned, sin entered the world. Adam's sin brought death, so death spread to everyone, for everyone sinned* (Romans 5:12).

Adam and Eve's sin corrupted the entire world, including plants, animals, and the natural environment. Sin corrupted their bodies and nature. The sinful nature was passed down to every generation. We are born with a natural inclination towards sin, and not one person has been able to resist this sin nature.

Romans 3:23 makes it clear, "For everyone has sinned; we all fall short of God's glorious standard." 1 John 1:8 reiterates this truth, "If we say we have no sin, we deceive ourselves, and the truth is not in us" (ESV).

We may think we're good people overall, but hopefully no one would honestly try to argue that he or she has never sinned. If you've told one lie, you've sinned. If you have ever lusted for anyone other than your spouse, you've sinned. If you have ever been hateful with your words, you've sinned. We have all sinned.

According to Romans 6:23, "the wages of sin is death." Death is the penalty and natural consequence of sin. People have a hard time wrapping their minds around this concept. Death seems like a harsh punishment for the sins they've committed because it's impossible for the human mind to comprehend the majesty or the holiness or the justice of God.

To put things in perspective, imagine walking up to a random person and punching him in the face. What would happen? You might get lucky and get told off or get punched in return. If the individual presses charges, you might have to do some anger management classes and community service. Now, imagine walking up and doing the same to a police officer. If you punch a police officer, you will see the inside of a jail. That action is a felony. You will need a much more expensive lawyer. Now, imagine walking up to a powerful dictator, in his own country, and punching *him* in the face. You, my friend, are a dead man. The only question is whether your death will be instantaneous or agonizingly slow.

Committing an offense against higher levels of authority brings steeper consequences. Imagine the consequences for offending an all-powerful God, one who created you and has complete power and authority over you. What is the consequence for offending and rejecting Him? The Bible tells us it's death.

BETTER THAN FAIR

God was more than fair in giving Adam and Eve a paradise with only one rule. He was completely justified in designing creation to work perfectly in His presence and to become corrupted when mankind rejected Him. He has every right to refuse to allow sin to enter His perfect and holy Kingdom. Since everyone has sinned, no one deserves entry into that perfect and eternal Kingdom. God cannot tolerate sin. It's not fair to expect God to lower His standards and corrupt His Kingdom to allow us to spend eternity with Him.

Thankfully, God is much more than fair—He is merciful. It wasn't fair that God the Father had to send His only Son to this world to die in order to pay the penalty for our sins, but that's exactly what our loving, merciful, grace-filled, Heavenly Father did.

John 3:16 tells it best.

For God so loved the world, that he gave his only Son, that whoever believes in him should not perish but have eternal life (ESV).

God sent his Son to earth. To bypass man's sin nature, God divinely formed a child in Mary's womb. This child, Jesus, lived a sinless life. He perfectly modeled what a life of love and devotion to God should look like.

Then Jesus gave His life to pay for our sins. He shed His blood on the cross, and His innocent blood covered our sins and paid the price we owed.

John wrote this about Jesus, "He himself is the sacrifice that atones for our sins—and not only our sins but the sins of all the world" (1 John 2:2).

It may seem hard to believe that the blood of one man could atone for the sins of billions of people. It is possible because Jesus was both a flesh and blood human being and the all-powerful God of creation. He could be pierced, and His blood could flow, but Jesus also had the power of the omnipotent, omnipresent, eternal God. As an eternal being, His sacrifice provided an eternal offering. His eternal blood has no problem covering every sin mankind commits.

> But our High Priest offered himself to God as a single sacrifice for sins, good for all time. Then he sat down in the place of honor at God's right hand. There he waits until his enemies are humbled and made a footstool under his feet. For by that one offering he forever made perfect those who are being made holy (Hebrews 10:12-14).

In response to His love and sacrifice, God asks us to do one thing to prove our love and devotion—to trust in Jesus Christ as our savior. God is still making it easy for us. Adam and Eve had only one rule to follow to keep paradise. We only have to take one step of faith to inherit paradise. That's *all*—have faith. Anyone who believes in Jesus with a saving faith will experience eternal life rather than eternal death.

SAVED BY FAITH

We don't have to slave away to earn salvation. There's no sin we can commit to lose our salvation. Our past doesn't prevent salvation. Our future mistakes won't remove salvation. Jesus paid for all of our sins, past, present, and future. We are saved by faith and faith alone.

Paul could not make salvation clearer.

We are made right with God by placing our faith in Jesus Christ. And this is true for everyone who believes, no matter who we are. For everyone has sinned; we all fall short of God's glorious standard. Yet God, with undeserved kindness, declares that we are righteous. He did this through Christ Jesus when he freed us from the penalty for our sins. For God presented Jesus as the sacrifice for sin. People are made right with God when they believe that Jesus sacrificed his life, shedding his blood. This sacrifice shows that God was being fair when he held back and did not punish those who sinned in times past, for

he was looking ahead and including them in
what he would do in this present time. God did
this to demonstrate his righteousness, for he
himself is fair and just, and he declares sinners
to be right in his sight when they believe in
Jesus. Can we boast then that we have done
anything to be accepted by God? No, because
our acquittal is not based on obeying the law.
It is based on faith. So we are made right with
God through faith and not by obeying the law
(Romans 3:22-28).

We are incapable of saving ourselves or making ourselves good enough for God. We depend on His grace and mercy, and because He loves us so much, He extends salvation to us.

Jesus did the work. He was mocked. He was beaten. He was whipped. He had a crown of thorns shoved onto his head. He had nails driven into his hands and feet. He was crucified on a cross for hours. He experienced the wrath of His Father as He bore our sins on His back. He died for us.

Three days later, He rose from the dead and conquered sin and death forever. His empty tomb and the witnesses to His resurrection are proof He can extend eternal life to us. All we must do is believe He is who He says He is and give Him our lives.

WORTH THROUGH CHRIST

Jesus' sacrifice brings incredibly good news. It should motivate us to draw closer to God and live for Him more. If you are feeling worthless or unqualified to do more for God, I challenge you to hold up those thoughts to the Gospel. You will find that those assumptions don't line up.

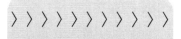

God knew every sin you would commit as a believer, and He chose you anyway.

If you are stressed about your past mistakes, keep in mind that those sins have been covered by the blood of Christ. Your sins did not catch God by surprise. He loved you before salvation and invited you to be part of His family despite your sin (Romans 5:8). God knew every sin you would commit as a believer, and He chose you anyway. He invited you to partner with Him despite your weaknesses. Avoiding failure isn't a prerequisite for Him calling us to ministry, because none of us would be in the ministry.

If you don't think you are good enough to serve, remind yourself that we aren't qualified because we're good. No one is good.

No one is righteous—not even one. No one is truly wise; no one is seeking God. All have turned away; all have become useless. No one does good, not a single one (Romans 3:10-12).

Fortunately, we don't have to remain in this unrighteous state. Because God changes our hearts. When we accept Jesus as our savior, we become a new creation in Christ and receive a new heart. With the power of the Holy Spirit working in our hearts, we can defeat our sin nature and accomplish great things for God. It is not us. It is God through us.

To say that we can't do great things for God is to assume that the accomplishments would be done in our own power, or to assume that God is not powerful enough to change our hearts and minds.

There are no question marks concerning God's ability to use us in the Kingdom of Heaven. Philippians 4:13 assures us that we can do all things through Christ's strength. Our loving Heavenly Father *wants* to spend more time with us and *wants* to partner with us in more meaningful ways.

The real question mark is whether we will let God work in us and through us.

SMALL GROUP DISCUSSION QUESTIONS

1. What was your favorite book or movie growing up? What attracted you to the story?

2. What aspects of the Gospel story make it a powerful and compelling narrative?

3. Has suffering in your life or in the world around you ever led you to question God? How did you question Him?

4. What are some effective ways to cope with suffering as a believer?

5. What do you think our response to the Gospel message should be? How should it affect our thoughts and actions?

Chapter 4
Evidence

For a brief time, I was in charge of interviewing and processing new volunteers at my church. One day, a young man dropped in to let me know he was interested in helping in the café we had in the lobby. We sold coffee, smoothies, and muffins to raise support for our missionary organization in Nicaragua. He seemed excited about being part of the team and pitching in to help the church. I gave him the application, along with a consent form for a background check, which I assured him is something we do for everyone that serves at church.

The moment I said background check, his demeanor changed. He seemed to shrink into his seat. With resignation in his voice, he told me that his background check wouldn't come back clean. He explained that a few years ago he'd gotten into an argument with his child's mother. He'd lost his temper and laid his hands on her. He scared her and caused some bruising before he came to his senses and stopped. His ex-girl-friend called the cops and had him arrested. He was charged with a domestic violence related offense and assigned anger management classes.

In that moment, this guy was baring his soul. This experience broke his relationship with his ex, lost him custody of his child, damaged his reputation, and marred his own identity. The shame of his sin and the pain he felt because of it was written all over his face and body language. This mistake motivated him to be a better person. When he walked through the doors of our church, he surrendered his heart to Jesus.

Now he felt like a new man and had been read-ing the Bible and getting more involved in church. That was why he wanted to volunteer in the café. With head down and defeat in his voice, he said, "But I guess that's not possible now. I'm sure you don't want to use me with that on my record."

Honestly, my initial reaction to his statement was to laugh. There is absolutely nothing funny about do-mestic violence. A man should never lay his hands on a woman in anger. But, I found it absurd to think that one act of violence, which occurred years before he came to know Jesus, would disqualify him from serv-ing muffins and smoothies in our café.

I was well aware of numerous volunteers and key leaders in our church who had done worse. God loves to use serious sinners to build His Kingdom.

Fortunately, I maintained some level of profession-alism and did not crack a smile. I felt my right cheek twitch a couple of times, but I fought it off. I assured him that, in Christ's eyes, his sin had been removed as far as the east is from the west, and we would be happy to have him serve in our café. Since then, I have had the pleasure of watching this young man grow and mature in his faith and understanding. He is now a key leader in our Men's Ministry program.

FLAWED OLD TESTAMENT HEROES

We struggle to believe God wants to use us despite our mistakes and weaknesses. Yet story after story in the Bible undermines this mindset. Noah got drunk, we're talking blackout, naked drunk, and then put a generational curse on his grandson because his son, Ham, gossiped about his drunkenness. God knew Noah would do this, yet he used him anyway.

Abraham, the father of God's chosen people, pimped out his wife … twice. For fear of his own safety, he claimed to be Sarah's brother rather than her husband, and he allowed two different kings to take her as their bride, accepting their gifts as a reward.

Moses, the greatest prophet and leader the nation of Israel has ever known, was a murderer with an apparent speech impediment. Samson was a weak-willed womanizer. King Solomon, the wisest man who ever lived, made Samson look like a Puritan. He had 700 wives and 300 concubines, and he allowed these women to turn his heart away from God. God knew he would commit these sins before Solomon was born, yet He still blessed Solomon with tremendous abilities and resources, and He allowed him to lead His people and write several books of the Bible.

Perhaps the quintessential example of God choosing people He knew would mess up is King David. David was a polygamist, an adulterer, a murderer, and a horrible father. Yet, God specifically chose him to be king and called David a man after God's own heart. Being called by God is not about what we've done in the past or will do in the future; it's about our heart's attitude and our desire to have a relationship with God and serve Him. God hates adultery and murder, but God used David's pain and brokenness to inspire some of the most powerful Psalms in the Bible. God brought forth even more purpose and redemption from the scandalous union between David and Bathsheba when He used their offspring, Solomon, to bring peace and prosperity to the kingdom. It is also through the line of David and Solomon that mankind received the ultimate redemption, the birth of Jesus, the Son of God. God can redeem any mistake and use it for His glory.

If Old Testament examples aren't enough to sway you, I've got plenty of New Testament examples to throw your way.

NEW TESTAMENT REDEMPTION

Outside of Peter, there really isn't enough info in the Gospels to get a good feel for the personality types of Jesus' twelve disciples. But, if his Gospel account is any indication, I would have gotten along with Matthew. The Gospel of Matthew is thorough, logical in its sequence, and focused—aspects I appreciate in a writer.

Matthew has an agenda in his Gospel, and I think it's two-fold. On one hand, he recounted his time with Jesus in a way that proved Jesus was the Messiah. Repeatedly, Matthew points out how Jesus' actions fulfilled one prophecy after another.

I believe his other purpose was to show that God called and used flawed people to build His Kingdom.

I find the genealogy that begins the book of Matthew hilarious. I know hilarious genealogy sounds like an oxymoron, but stay with me here. The Jews were a proud people who obsessed over ancestry and connecting their lineage back to Abraham. Women were rarely included in genealogies. They were second-class citizens with few rights, and only fathers and sons were listed. But Matthew mentions several mothers in his opening genealogy.

He never mentions Sarah, the mother of the faith or Rebekah, the mother of Jacob and grandmother to the 12 tribes of Israel. No, Matthew only includes women who Jews would have been embarrassed to mention.

He mentions Tamar, who dressed up like a prostitute to seduce her father-in-law Judah. Their union produced a son named Perez. He mentions Rahab, who actually was a prostitute, a Canaanite prostitute. He mentions Ruth, who was a destitute, Moabite widow.

When Matthew lists King David, he mentions both Bathsheba (with whom David committed adultery) and Uriah (the man David murdered to cover up his adultery).

Why does Matthew go out of his way to list these people? Because he wanted to show the Jews, who cared so much about their paternal ancestry and "pure" bloodlines, that God used women to accomplish His purposes, women of different races and nationalities, women who had committed egregious sins. God chose them, redeemed them, and used them to write His story.

Why is Matthew interested in proving that God can use people who others deem worthless? It's because he knows exactly how that feels. Matthew was called out of the tax collecting business, a business that was as disreputable to the Jews as any profession. Most tax collectors were greedy cheats, and it's highly unlikely Matthew was an exception. After Jesus invited Matthew to follow Him, Matthew invited Jesus into his home for a meal. In Matthew 9, Matthew's friends are described as "disreputable sinners," and the Pharisees refer to them as "scum." If Matthew's friends are all disreputable sinners and scum, it's pretty safe to assume that Matthew was no angel.

I believe that's why Matthew writes the way he does. He understands God can use those who have sullied their names. Hyper-aware of the unbelievable grace and mercy God showed him, he is much more prone to show grace and mercy to others. When he writes, he describes human failings with transparency and grace.

Matthew's portrayal of John the Baptist, who was known as a great prophet of almost mythical proportions, focuses on John's humanity. Matthew recounts how, in a moment of weakness while sitting in prison, John the Baptist sent his disciples to Jesus to question whether He really was the Messiah. Jesus responded with grace and refers to John the Baptist as the great-est man who has ever lived.

Matthew also includes a detailed account of John the Baptist's death—a death that seems so tragic and pointless. It's not pointless, though. It's completely consistent with the theme of the Bible. It's not about us; it's all about Jesus. As John the Baptist attests in John 3:30 "He must become greater and greater, and I must become less and less." When we minimize our importance, God uses us and exalts us. When we inflate our value, God pulls away and humbles us.

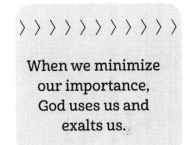

When we minimize our importance, God uses us and exalts us.

Matthew portrays Jesus' tendency to show grace to humble sinners and rail against proud leaders. I don't think it's a coincidence that Matthew provides the most grace-filled version of Jesus' teachings on divorce, while also including passage after passage of Jesus ripping into and calling out the Pharisees. If you think that you're in perfect shape to be used by God, you probably aren't. If you think that you're not worthy to be used by God, you're probably ready to start.

This is why Jesus chose the disciples He did, and why they were so effective. Without the religious pedigree or the typical ministry gifts of Pharisees, the disciples felt unqualified to do ministry work on their own. That feeling of unworthiness made them extremely grateful for the opportunity and much more likely to rely on Jesus' leadership.

It is amazing what God can accomplish through us when we don't make ministry about us. When we embrace this mentality, God can overcome any mistake. This is how Peter, a fisherman who suggested worshipping Moses and Elijah, who tried to prevent Jesus' work on the cross, who cut off the ear of a temple servant, and then denied even knowing Jesus three times, could be tasked with starting God's Church and leading thousands of people to Christ at Pentecost. Also how a murderer like Paul could become the greatest missionary in church history and author thirteen of the twenty-seven books of the New Testament. His past and reputation inspired him to strive harder than anyone as an offering to God for the unbelievable grace God had shown him. God's grace also transformed Mary Magdalene, a woman who was demon possessed. God made her an important figure in Jesus' circle and gifted her with the honor of being the first witness to Jesus' resurrection.

MODERN DAY REDEMPTION

I love these Bible stories, but some of my favorite stories of God's ability to redeem are the ones I've witnessed in our church. Two individuals that immediately come to my mind are Kyle and Janelle, and both have graciously agreed to let me share their testimonies.

Kyle didn't grow up in church. He was a military brat who moved from place to place, which made it difficult to forge healthy friendships. He found his identity in sports and dreamed of becoming a professional baseball player. When a shoulder injury took away his one passion, he turned to partying to fill the void. He started with alcohol and marijuana, and at just 15 years old, spent most of his nights sneaking into bars and getting wasted.

He found new friends, which led to selling weed and sampling stronger drugs. He experimented with roofies and tranquilizers, but it was his introduction to cocaine that changed his life. One of his cocaine buddies had a rich uncle who was a cocaine distributor. So, Kyle graduated to cocaine dealer and started selling massive amounts of the drug.

Suddenly, Kyle had plenty of cash to keep the party going all night long, and he became a prominent figure in the nightclub scene. He was only 17. His life as a serious drug dealer became increasingly dangerous. He lost several close friends to overdoses and gunshots, and one night, he nearly joined them. A former friend put a hit on him, and he narrowly escaped the hail of bullets. This near-death experience freaked him out, and his family moved to North Carolina to escape the violence and get a fresh start.

Old habits die hard, though. Kyle quickly found a new rough crowd to hang with and graduated to even more dangerous crimes. At 19 he was charged with armed robbery and assault with a deadly weapon. He spent two years in jail.

Released from jail at 21, Kyle knew he never wanted to go back to prison, but he also didn't have the strength to change his ways. He kept going back to doing drugs, and he kept losing jobs. When he was out of work, he would resort to dealing drugs, which would lead to more crime and violence. The result was homelessness. He had burnt so many bridges that even his mother refused to take him in, convinced that he could never change his ways.

Through the tough love and grace of a counselor at a homeless shelter, Kyle opened his heart to Jesus. All the years of stress and pain and shame melted away. The road through rehab and to recovery and stability was not easy, but with the power of the Holy Spirit now inside him, he had the strength to see it through.

He is now a godly husband and father, and one of our Hospitality Team leaders. We love having him as a volunteer leader at our church, but his true calling isn't found at our church. Kyle established a nonprofit organization called Next Steps Today, which provides housing, counseling, accountability, and resources for addicts. He is bringing healing and purpose and opportunity to those who made the same mistakes he did. The fruit of God's work in Kyle is evident every Sunday as a group of former addicts attends church clean and sober.

OVERCOMING PAIN AND FINDING PURPOSE

Janelle grew up in church, but not a church that would inspire a love for God. At 5 years old, Janelle's church-going father began sexually abusing her. He used God's name and fear of His wrath to manipulate her into keeping quiet about the abuse and allowing it to go on. At age 8, her dad started inviting his friends over and insisting that she give herself to them, too. At age 12, one of the youth leaders in her church, the man who helped her get baptized, walked in the door to have his chance at sexually assaulting her.

Janelle hated God. It's hard to blame her when the men in her life, the ones who were supposed to model for her what her Heavenly Father was like, abused her instead. Janelle started cutting early in life in order to release some of her pain. When she got older, she tried filling the void in her life with sex and alcohol. Unable to trust men, she moved from partner to partner, self-destructing the relationships with promiscuous behavior.

One of her many boyfriends invited her to church. Understandably, she was rather hesitant. Still quite angry with God, she wanted nothing to do with Him or church, but she gave in. This church was different from any she had been to. There was a culture of love and acceptance, and the teaching was both engaging and inspiring. Her relationship with the guy did not last, but her relationship with our body of believers did. Eventually, she partnered with one of our female teachers and worked through a Bible study on healing from sexual abuse. Before long, Janelle, who had been so angry at God, came to understand His great love for her, and she accepted Him as her savior.

What I've shared of her story is a very sanitized version and only the tip of the iceberg of all she has experienced and endured. It took years for her to gain the upper hand in the battle against her demons and maintain a life of purity and devotion to God. But her story has been an inspiration to hundreds of people, and the fruit in her life is abundant.

She joined a mission team to Managua, Nicaragua to minister to the women and children of House of Hope, which is a Christ-centered nonprofit that seeks to rescue women (and their children) from a life of prostitution in third world countries, providing them with safe living spaces and an alternate means of earning income. We shared our love and resources with the women and children there, did some maintenance work for them, and led them in a time of worship. After one worship set, Janelle gave her testimony to the ladies of House of Hope. Her story moved them to tears and opened their hearts. At the end of her testimony, they came forward and wrapped their arms around her, wept with her, and thanked her. Many made life-changing decisions that day, decisions to give their pain and suffering to God. Imagine a story that would move and break the hearts of women who have worked in some of the most dangerous brothels in the entire world.

Since then, Janelle has plugged into our church. She has led worship, served as a children's service coordinator, and acted as assistant summer camp director. She has a heart for Jesus and a heart for serving that keeps growing.

God has provided story after story, both in the Bible and in the church, to show us He can use us despite our circumstances. He can use us despite our pasts, despite our mistakes, and despite our weaknesses. God revels in using us in our weakness, and we won't be ready to be used by God *until* we recognize we are full of mistakes and weaknesses. Once we embrace our failings and open our hearts to God, He will take care of the rest.

SMALL GROUP DISCUSSION QUESTIONS

1. What are your favorite redemption stories in
    the Bible?

2. What is your favorite redemption story within
    your community?

3. If you had to compile a list of the top
    qualifications God looks for in someone He
    calls to do His work, what would you include?

4. What are the takeaways we should hold on to
    when we consider all the broken people God
    has used to do great things?

5. What can we do to prepare ourselves for
    when God asks us to do something for His
    Kingdom?

Chapter 5
Ministry Musts

I wish I could have witnessed Jesus' Sermon on the Mount. I can only imagine the dumbfounded looks on people in the audience. Jesus' sermon points were revolutionary, turning everything people thought at the time upside down.

His sermon points are not random. He lists each blessing in the natural order a person becomes a believer and grows into maturity.

First, we must recognize our need for God.

Blessed are the poor in spirit, for theirs is the kingdom of heaven (Matthew 5:3 ESV).

Then, God comforts us who mourn, especially if we are broken over our sin.

Blessed are those who mourn, for they shall be comforted (Matthew 5:4).

It is when we humble ourselves and repent that we will inherit the earth.

Blessed are the meek, for they shall inherit the earth (Matthew 5:5).

Once we are changed by the saving power of Jesus, our heart longs for justice and righteousness.

Blessed are those who hunger and thirst for righteousness (Matthew 5:6).

Then we are much more willing to show mercy.

Blessed are the merciful, for they shall obtain mercy (Matthew 5:7).

As we grow in understanding and maturity, we also grow in sanctification, becoming pure in heart.

When we seek to bring peace and unity, Satan will do everything he can to hinder. Through this persecution, we are reminded to be happy and rejoice because our reward will be greater.

Blessed are you when they revile and persecute you, and say all kinds of evil against you falsely for my sake (Matthew 5:11).

The crucial application I want to highlight is found in verse 3, "God blesses those who are poor and realize their need for him" (my paraphrase). The poverty mentioned here is spiritual poverty. It's a recognition that we are empty and broken, and only God can fill and heal our lives. Recognizing your need for God is the first step in finding relationship and redemption with Him.

When I was teaching English, I formed a friendship with a colleague. We often talked about our classes and literature while sharing a lunch or playing a few sets of tennis. Whenever I could slip it in, we also talked about religion and God. He was a skeptic, and I became more and more burdened to help him see the truth. I challenged him to send me every skeptical thought or question he had. I was convinced I could win him over with my eloquent, logical arguments. So we debated back and forth for months.

While he conceded my arguments had merit and supporting evidence, he just couldn't wrap his mind around the idea that God would send him to hell for the life he lived. By the world's standards, he was a saint. He was kind and considerate. He poured his time, energy, and wisdom into his students and made a difference. He lived a moral life free of harmful vices. Simply put, he did not feel a *need* for God.

By the end of our debates, I found myself wishing something really bad would happen to him. I know that sounds horrible, but please understand my desire for some pain and suffering to enter his life did not come from a place of anger or frustration. It came from a place of love and concern. I was worried that if he continued to go through life without any tragic circumstances or harsh consequences to sin, he might leave this world never knowing his creator.

My friend had never experienced tragedy or loss. The benefits of his many talents and comfortable circumstances left him content with his life. He was on a path that led to eternal death, but he was not spiritually poor enough to see it.

BLIND TO THEIR NEED

It seems successful, socially conscious people are difficult to lead to Christ. Perhaps because they have chosen, unwittingly and for their own personal reasons, to align their lives with a number of God's commands. They are hard-working, ethical, generous, and caring. God has designed this world to thrive when we follow his commands, and plenty of unbelievers are unintentionally living out God's standards. As a result, they are successful in most of their pursuits and relationships, and while they don't feel completely fulfilled, there's no gaping void in their lives that they are desperate to fill. Because they are obeying the second most important commandment (to love people), they don't recognize their need to follow the most important commandment (to love God).

It's dangerous to do the right thing for the wrong reasons. Doing so will harden your heart toward God, turn your focus inward, and leave you content with values that won't last.

The Pharisees were maniacal about following every command in the Mosaic Law, except the two most important—love God with all your heart and love people as much as you love yourself. They were so focused on earning their way to heaven they added man-made traditions to the Mosaic Law, making their religious code even harder to follow. They believed their strict religious code made them worthy of eternal life.

When Jesus called their actions meaningless because they lacked love, he rocked their world. Pharisees thought they could earn the right to heaven through good deeds. Jesus came to proclaim deeds are filthy rags in the eyes of God. The only path to eternal life is through realizing you couldn't possibly be good enough to deserve heaven. It is only through grace and the sacrifice of Jesus Christ that we are made right with God. This teaching threatened the Pharisees' self-image, and they got rid of Jesus rather than change their identity.

The story of the blind man in John 9 illustrates this dichotomy between recognizing your need for God and being blind to it. I strongly encourage you to read the full account. It is brilliant, hilarious, and encouraging.

Here is a synopsis of the story: Jesus came across a man who was blind since birth. Jesus' disciples asked whether this man was born blind because of his sins or his parents' sins. (What egregious sins this guy could have committed inside his mother's womb, I'm not sure, but this is how people thought when they saw infirmities in others.) Jesus told them this man was born blind so God could be glorified through him. Then Jesus spit on the ground, made a little mud mask, and spread it over the man's eyes. After the man washed off the mud, his dead eyes could see.

It's an incredible display of God's power. The community must have started dancing in the streets, right? Wrong. The people were confused. Jesus performed this miracle on a Sabbath. Healing and making mud on a Sabbath—that was breaking two religious laws. Could God be behind such an act?

The formerly blind guy was brought to the Pharisees, where he delivered a brief, yet powerful testimony. The Pharisees claimed Jesus must be a horrible sinner since he broke their Sabbath traditions. The formerly blind man responded, "I don't know about all that, but what I do know is that I was blind and now I can see" (my paraphrase).

The Pharisees didn't like that response and badgered him with more questions. Then comes my favorite part of the story. The formerly blind beggar taught the Pharisees about God. To fully appreciate the irony and significance of this situation, keep in mind that a couple of hours before, this man knew no other life than complete destitution and dependence on others. His whole identity was wrapped up in appearing as pathetic as possible to draw the sympathy of people passing by.

Jesus changes everything. An hour before, this man acted completely helpless, and an hour after he boldly defended his faith and out-debated the top religious leaders in the community. Unable to refute his points with logic or Scripture, the Pharisees called him names and kicked him out of the synagogue.

Then Jesus appeared to the former blind man again and revealed He is the Messiah. The man's immediate response was to declare his faith and worship Jesus. The purpose of this Gospel narrative is summed up by Jesus' next statement.

I entered this world to render judgment—to give sight to the blind and to show those who think they see that they are blind (John 9:39).

The blind beggar was made whole because he recognized his need for God and humbly allowed God to work on him. The Pharisees remained broken because they were blind to their flaws, failed to see their need for salvation, and refused to allow God to work on their hard hearts.

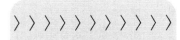

You cannot serve God effectively if you are self-reliant or proud.

According to Jesus' sermon on the mount, it is the poor in spirit who will inherit the kingdom of heaven and the humble who will inherit the earth. If you want this inheritance, it is absolutely necessary to humble yourself and rely on God. Relying on God and staying humble are also ministry musts. You cannot serve God effectively if you are self-reliant or proud.

SPIRITUAL PRIDE VS SPIRITUAL POVERTY

When I got divorced, I believed I was forever disqualified for significant ministry work. God opened my eyes to reveal the truth. *Until* I went through my divorce, I was unqualified to serve in full-time ministry.

Before my divorce, what I saw in the mirror was a moral, talented, successful guy who had life figured out. I was confident and self-reliant, taking great pride in my abilities and reputation. These characteristics made me darn near worthless for ministry use. I stayed active in church and shared my faith on occasion, but I did it on my terms. As a result, I didn't bear much fruit.

Even my siblings who looked up to me shied away from coming to me with their problems. After my divorce, I found out that a few of my siblings struggled with some significant sin problems. I was shocked that they could go through such experiences without me knowing. I asked them why they hadn't confided in me. Their response was that before my divorce, I wasn't approachable or relatable. They assumed I wouldn't understand and I would judge them. My spiritual pride turned people away.

After my divorce, humility wasn't a problem. The man I saw in the mirror was a worthless loser who was barely holding on by clinging to God and leaning on the support of my church, my family, and the one close friend who stuck by my side.

It was in this frame of mind that ministry opportunities started popping up. I went from attendee to volunteer to life group leader to Bible study teacher to pastor to preacher in a three-year time period. I felt completely unworthy of each invitation to do more for God's church, which made it a lot easier to be thankful for God's blessings and give Him the glory for my successes. Humility changes a leader.

Moses is known for being Israel's greatest Old Testament leader, and the Bible tells us he was "very humble—more humble than any other person on earth" (Numbers 12:3). I think D. L. Moody summed up Moses's ministry best: "Moses spent forty years in the king's palace thinking that he was somebody; then he lived forty years in the wilderness finding out that without God he was a nobody; finally he spent forty more years discovering how a nobody with God can be a somebody." I want to be a nobody, too. It is far better to be a nobody who God uses to do something eternal than to think you're somebody and accomplish nothing meaningful.

USING OUR MISTAKES

Humility wasn't the only positive takeaway from my pain and disgrace. My divorce opened doors I never anticipated. My pain and humiliation made me relatable and approachable to many more people. Broken people loved having the option of going to the divorced pastor for help. They figured I could relate to their pain, and as far as anyone can understand another person's pain, I could. My painful experiences helped me empathize with others and better equipped me to advise and encourage them.

The more transparency I showed, the more people gravitated towards my teaching. The more I revealed my failings, the more others confessed theirs. And, as my senior pastor is fond of saying, "God won't heal what we hide." We must acknowledge our sins, hand them over to God, and let Him heal and use them. In His hands, our sins are not a detriment. They can be used for His glory. That is the message of Romans 8:28.

And we know that God causes everything to work together for the good of those who love God and are called according to his purpose for them.

God is working constantly, and he redeems the mistakes of His children. The actions Satan intended for evil, God uses for good. His good plans for us are not second rate plans because of our sin. God's plan B is just as good as His plan A. I am living proof. I am happily remarried to an amazing woman, and I

> **God's plan B is just as good as His plan A.**

have two wonderful sons. I am the teaching pastor at a thriving church. I wouldn't trade my life for anyone else's. I don't know what my life would have been like if I had made better choices as a young adult, but it's hard for me to imagine a life more fulfilling than the one I have. As long as we rely on God and stay humble, there is no limit to God's power to redeem us.

Failures and weaknesses are blessings in disguise. They keep us humble and dependent on Jesus. Three times, Paul begged the Lord to take away the source of his pain and suffering. Each time, God's response was, "My grace is all you need. My power works best in weakness" (2 Corinthians 12:9). In our weakness, we rely on God's power and keep our focus on Him. When we rely on our strength, we are tempted to take the credit and glory for ourselves.

If you are feeling unworthy and inadequate to partner with God, you are in the right frame of mind to be called. God loves to use humble people. All you have to do is say yes to Him working in you and through you.

SMALL GROUP DISCUSSION QUESTIONS

1. Who has had the most impact on your walk with Christ? What character traits stick out in those people?

2. Name a person who you wish would accept Jesus as their savior? What do you think is holding them back?

3. What are you doing to point people to Jesus?

4. Who is someone in your circle of influence who demonstrates humility? How do they show this character trait?

5. Describe a time when you felt completely powerless and had to rely on God. What did you learn from the experience?

6. What are some action steps we can take to become more humble?

Chapter 6
Ministry Killer

I grew up in a family that thrived on competition. My dad was a sports nut. Ok, that's underselling it. He lived and breathed sports, spending almost all of his free time watching sports, playing sports, or training us how to play sports. I developed an intense competitive streak and became obsessed with winning. When I say that I hated to lose, I mean it. Losing filled me with rage and self-loathing. I never wanted to stop playing until I came out on top.

I took extreme pride in being the best, and if I wasn't good at something, I avoided it. I had to be the best, and I had to make sure it was perfectly clear to everyone else that I was the best.

My competitiveness knew no bounds, even as a long-term substitute at a local middle school.

I filled in for a semester in the Special Education department. Back when schools would separate the Special Education kids from the mainstream students. (Fortunately, this practice is now frowned upon.) I was blessed with an incredibly sweet class of ID (intellectually disabled) and TBI (traumatic brain injury) students. At recess, all the Special Education classes went out to play together, and the biggest draw was the one basketball hoop. The kids begged me to play, and I always gave in, despite my dress shoes and khaki pants. I was pretty good at basketball, but I would just fool around on the court with the kids, rarely using energy or leaving my feet.

One day, a couple of the kids started talking trash to me. (I would just like to point out that these kids were in the Special Education department because of emotional disabilities, not physical disabilities. This story is already going to make me look bad enough. I don't need you envisioning heart-wrenching videos you've seen from the Special Olympics.) They started saying stuff like, "Mr. Thompson, you're tall, but that's all you got. You can't play. You can't hang with us. We could crush you one on one." At first, I laughed and said, "Is that right?" Before long, I started telling them that not only could I beat them one on one, I could beat them three on one. That taunt got them riled up, and my challenge was accepted immediately.

I tried my best to take it easy and give them a chance. I really did. But the kids started talking trash when they scored, "You ain't nothing, Mr. Thompson. I own you. You can't handle me."

And that was all it took.

I started to play for real. I let the mouthiest kid go around me, so when he went up for a layup I could block his shot in dramatic fashion. I smacked the ball so hard that it rebounded off the side of the school building and nearly took a kid's head off. The kids watching went "Ooooooooooo" and began laughing at the kid. I blocked every shot and stole almost every pass from these three kids. On offense, I dribbled between their legs and finished with acrobatic layups. I crushed them and mercilessly embarrassed them.

Why?

Because I was too proud to allow a school yard of overlooked Special Education kids think they were anywhere near as good as I was.

Is there any doubt I needed some humbling?

THE COST OF PRIDE

If we held a contest to determine the one sin that is most detrimental to God's Kingdom, the winner would be pride—the father of all sins. Pride got Satan cast out of heaven when he recruited angels to serve him rather than God. Pride led Eve to eat the fruit from the forbidden tree because she desired to be like God. Pride led Cain to kill Abel as he allowed his shame and rejection turn into murderous hate. Noah cursed his grandson, causing generations of pain over one embarrassment. Mankind built a tower at Babel so they could reach heaven without God. God punished this act of arrogance by confusing their language, leading to the racial and national schisms we've endured throughout history. Look how much damage pride has caused, and we've only listed the actions of people in one-fourth of the first book of the Bible.

The book of Proverbs helps us gain an understanding of how God views the sin of pride. Here are a few verses on the topic:

The Lord detests all the proud of heart. Be sure of this: They will not go unpunished
(Proverbs 16:5 NIV).

Pride goes before destruction, and haughtiness before a fall
(Proverbs 16:18).

Haughty eyes and a proud heart—the unplowed field of the wicked—produce sin
(Proverbs 21:4 NIV).

Pride is the path that leads to sin and destruction. Pride prevents people from being used by God in the first place, and pride destroys the ministry work of those who are currently used by God.

PRIDE PREVENTING MINISTRY

Countless believers attend church, but do little for the church because of pride. They are saying no to the Holy Spirit's promptings because they are worried about what people will think of them. They don't want to reveal their past or admit their lack of biblical understanding. It's tragic to think of all the CEOs, managers, entrepreneurs, professors, doctors, lawyers, and politicians who refuse to do God's work because they're used to being in charge and won't work less prestigious jobs. Unbelievably gifted men and women, from all walks of life, waste their God-given talents on work that will pass away rather than work that will last for eternity.

Church culture helps us become pros at pretending. A typical Sunday morning might include waking up with a hangover, getting in a heated argument with your spouse over an insensitive comment, or yelling at your kids for making you late, but once we walk through that church door, it's all toothy smiles and godly clichés.

This holy façade is fostered from the top down. Church leaders project an aura of righteousness they don't feel or possess. They struggle with anger and pride and lust and fear and worry and bitterness just like the members in their congregation, but come Sunday morning, they put on the mask of sainthood.

James offers a better way to live, "Confess your sins to each other and pray for each other so that you may be healed" (James 5:16a). Only through transparency and confession can we find the support and healing we need.

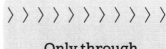

Only through transparency and confession can we find the support and healing we need.

Ironically, the church members who fail to heed James's advice the most might be senior pastors. With their lofty positions, they feel the most pressure to hide their flaws. They are also the least likely to have true accountability in their lives. God help them if they are excellent leaders and communicators because the likely result is their churches will grow, their wealth will increase, and they will be showered with praise. If they aren't careful, the praise and the accomplishments will make them proud, and they will start making self-serving decisions.

It is shocking how many mega-church pastors have plummeted from the highest rungs of church ministry. They have fallen for various reasons, some over money scandals, some over sex scandals, some over abuses of power, and some for overall abusive behavior. I believe the root cause of each scandal has been pride.

These great leaders in the church became so popular, so praised, and so powerful that they made ministry more about what they wanted than what God wanted. They convinced themselves that the ministry couldn't survive without them, which emboldened their actions. Eventually, these leaders deceived themselves into believing they could get away with certain sins or even that they deserved certain allowances.

Those around them enabled them, looking away and ignoring warning signs until the only recourse was a public scandal. The result is always a mass exodus, a broken and disillusioned remnant, and a severely tarnished legacy.

While these scandals have shocked the church world, they really shouldn't come as a big surprise. Men and women who have praise, success, and power heaped on them are the most likely to struggle with pride.

I am not bashing mega-church pastors. I admire many of them, and a few of them have had a crucial impact on my personal walk with Christ. My heart goes out to the ones who have fallen. I don't assume that I could have handled their situations better. I believe I would have succumbed to sinful temptations even faster if I had experienced the pride-inducing success they did.

The love and redemption we've discussed is available to former superstar pastors, too. God can redeem every situation. If David could continue to serve God as King and write Psalms after what he did, then there's a significant role for us all. Only pride will keep us on the sidelines. Humility will heal us and make us effective.

When we embrace our weaknesses and give God the credit, He uses us for His glory. When we become proud and take the credit for our accomplishments, He leaves us to our own devices, and we fall.

GIDEON'S RISE AND FALL

One of the best biblical illustrations of this principle is the story of Gideon. When God first appeared to Gideon, Gideon was hiding in a winepress, quietly separating kernels of wheat, terrified the Midianites would find him and steal his food. When God announced His intention to use Gideon to save the nation of Israel from Midian's oppression, Gideon was incredulous. He protested that he was the least respected person in his father's family, and his family's clan was the least respected clan in his tribe of Israel. Gideon felt grossly underqualified, and it took several miracles before God convinced Gideon he could save Israel.

Gideon rallied 32,000 soldiers to combat 135,000 Midianites. This put a nobody from a lesser tribe of Israel in charge of an army outnumbered 4 to 1. But God knew the odds weren't steep enough to ensure only He would receive the credit for victory. God told Gideon to send the frightened soldiers home and then sent a bunch of others home because of the way they drank water. Gideon was left with 300 soldiers to face 135,000. You would think 450 to 1 odds would suffice—but wait, there's more. The soldiers were instructed to use no weapons for this battle. Each one was to take a trumpet in one hand and a jar with a torch in the other.

In the middle of the night, the Israelites blew their trumpets, smashed their jars, held up their torches, and shouted, "A sword for the Lord and for Gideon!" The Midianites awoke in a panic and fought each other. They wiped themselves out and left a remnant for the Israelites to chase down. Israel was saved by the mighty power of God. The victory began with one humble man saying yes to God.

It is rare for pastors or Sunday school teachers to teach on the rest of Gideon's story. It's much more encouraging to finish the story on a high note, but I think the destruction of Gideon's legacy is a cautionary tale worth noting. After Gideon led Israel to victory over the Midianites, they tried to make him ruler. He wisely declined and pointed out that the Lord rules. But he felt he deserved a portion of the spoils of war. The amount he received was the equivalent of over 40 pounds of gold. He made an ephod (priestly garment) with the gold. Before long, Israelites began making pilgrimages to worship this ephod.

Gideon made a sacred ephod from the gold and put it in Ophrah, his hometown. But soon all the Israelites prostituted themselves by worshiping it, and it became a trap for Gideon and his family (Judges 8:27).

Gideon accepted the worship that belongs only to God. He used the fame he received from being an instrument of God to amass praise, worship, wealth, and wives for himself. We're not told how many wives Gideon took for himself, but it had to be quite the harem, because he had 70 sons. 70. That number doesn't even include his daughters. I can't even imagine that home life.

Gideon should have left an incredible family legacy, but that is not what happened. Gideon had two more sons, including one born to a concubine. (Apparently, his many wives still weren't enough for him.) This son was named Abimelech. He hired a bunch of renegades and killed all 70 of his older brothers.

What a tragic ending to a wonderful children's Bible story. God didn't want Gideon's children killed. God was sickened by Abimelech's actions. Later, when a woman tossed a millstone off a tower and crushed Abimelech's skull, killing him, the Bible says it was God's way of paying him back for his atrocities. God didn't want Gideon to steal God's honor and glory by setting up an idol for worship, either. Sin has consequences. Sin pushes God's protection away and provides Satan with the opening to attack us.

Gideon, as a humble man who relied on God, built an incredible legacy that inspired believers for thousands of years. Gideon, as a proud man who made self-serving decisions, tarnished his legacy and destroyed his family. We miss out on God's good plans for us when we focus on either our failures or our successes. Our sole focus should be on making choices that serve God rather than self. We need to cling to the thought that life is not about us.

IT'S NOT ABOUT US

If you don't think you're worthy of serving in the church, remind yourself that it's not about you. If you are worried about what other people will think, remind yourself that it's not about you. And if you find success in your ministry work, remind yourself it's not about you. It is all about God.

All honor and glory to God forever and ever!
He is the eternal King, the unseen one who
never dies. He alone is God. Amen
(1 Timothy 1:17).

God is worthy of all honor and glory. If you try to steal His honor and glory, He will ensure your fall. If you humble yourself and give Him the honor and glory He deserves, He will lift you up and bestow honor and glory on you. This universal principle is at odds with our human nature and seems counterintuitive, but Jesus designed this world and His Kingdom to work with this principle.

Jesus scolded the Pharisees for seeking glory in Matthew 23.

The greatest among you must be a servant. But those who exalt themselves will be humbled, and those who humble themselves will be exalted (v. 11).

When Jesus' disciples argued over which of them would be the greatest, Jesus explained that His Kingdom works differently.

Those who are the greatest among you should take the lowest rank, and the leader should be like a servant (Luke 22:26).

It is difficult to resist the temptations of pride because it comes at us from so many angles and directions. Even when we've kept our pride in check, our success can lead to pride in our humble reputation.

But when we step back and look at the big picture, we realize how ludicrous it is to be proud. God created us. We had no hand in deciding how our genetic development would proceed. Our physical abilities, appearances, spiritual gifts, family dynamics, and life opportunities are all gifts from God. (I'm guessing a few of you don't see some of these things as gifts, but you'll have to take that up with God. I had nothing to do with it.)

James 1:17a says,

Every good gift and every perfect gift is from above, coming down from the Father of lights (ESV).

Every good thing in your life is a gift from God. All of your accomplishments and resources are gifts from God. He deserves all the credit. When we own this reality, it makes it a lot easier to maintain an attitude of gratefulness, generosity, and humility.

OUR MODEL FOR HUMILITY

The key to maintaining the right attitude is to keep our eyes on the perfect model for such a life. Jesus' humility will never cease to blow my mind. How can an all-powerful, all-knowing, all-present God be humble? How can someone who spoke the universe into existence willingly enter that same universe as a helpless baby? How did he endure submitting to the authority of flawed parents and clueless religious leaders? Understanding the full extent of who He was and all that He would do for mankind, why was His natural reaction to wash His disciples' feet, like a lowly servant? How did He resist calling on 10,000 angels or revealing His true power when the Jewish leaders and Roman soldiers mocked Him, spit on Him, whipped Him, and ultimately crucified Him? How could Jesus be so humble?

There's no better proof for the Trinity than God's love and humility. How could God know love or prove to be humble if He existed in isolation? For love and humility to be part of His nature, God must have had equals to demonstrate these qualities. Long before the creation of angels or this universe, God the Father, God the Son, and God the Holy Spirit had each other to love and serve.

We see evidence of this love and service relationship throughout John's Gospel. The first chapter reveals that Jesus created the universe and everything in it. He is the source of life for mankind. Jesus created mankind because His Father wanted children with whom He could extend His love. Jesus created us to serve and please His Father. He also fulfilled the plan of redemption so God the Father could adopt us as His children. Jesus' purpose on earth was to serve His Father.

For I have come down from heaven, not to do my own will but the will of him who sent me (John 6:38).

In response to His Son's obedience and sacrifice, the Father made Jesus Lord over everything, seating Him on a throne, and bestowing on Him all honor and glory.

The Holy Spirit serves as a helper and living testimony to this beautiful plan between Father and Son. As early as the second verse in the Bible, God the Spirit hovers over creation, bearing witness to the work of the Son. The Spirit was there to testify at Jesus' baptism, which began His earthly ministry, and He was there to raise Jesus from the dead at the end of His earthly ministry.

Shortly before His death, Jesus amazed His disciples by telling them they would be better off without Him because the Spirit is coming (John 16:7-15). Jesus honors the Holy Spirit's power and purpose in this passage. Simply stated, the Holy Spirit's purpose is to point people to Jesus.

But I will send you the Advocate—the Spirit of truth. He will come to you from the Father and will testify all about me (John 15:26).

Father, Son, and Spirit display a perpetual cycle of love and humility through service to one another. This is who They are, and They designed a world that works best when mankind aligns itself with these two essential qualities. It is better to love. It is better to serve.

THE POWER OF HUMILITY

Humility is not weakness. It is choosing to withhold strength to show love and service. Being humble is a better way of living. I was introduced to humility by my grandfather. One day, I overheard my mother talking with her sister about their dad's skill in playing checkers. They rehashed his reputation as the best checkers player in the county and how he would win every tournament. As an eight-year-old boy, I felt the need to correct my mom concerning grandpa's checker playing skills. I piped up, "Mom, grandpa wasn't good at checkers. I beat him all the time." Mom patted her naïve son on the leg and revealed the hard truth. "Honey, he let you win."

As a boy, I was skeptical because it was incomprehensible to me to let someone else win. As a man, I have no doubts grandpa let me win, and his generosity is why I cherish those memories of playing checkers with him. If he had crushed me like he could, I would have hated playing with him. I don't have many memories of my grandpa since he died while I was young, but I remember his gentle humility.

People enjoy being around humble people. People listen to humble people. God will use humble people. If the God of creation can humble Himself, then we have no excuse. By swallowing our pride and constantly reminding ourselves of God's love, we can leave a lasting legacy that will shape the lives around us and grow God's Kingdom.

SMALL GROUP DISCUSSION QUESTIONS

1. How would you describe pride?

2. Have you ever made a poor decision because of your pride? If so, and you don't mind sharing, share an example with the group.

3. Why do you think so many people allow themselves to walk down the destructive path of pride?

4. Pride is a sin that is rarely confronted because it's subtle and doesn't seem as bad as some other sins, even though it is one of the most dangerous sins. What are some signs that a person is struggling with a pride issue?

5. What can we do to guard ourselves against becoming proud or arrogant?

Chapter 7
Missing

My parents did their best to keep us kids from negative influences. So, I spent my elementary and
middle school years in a small Christian school. When
my baby sister was born, kid number five, my parents
finally waved the white flag and chose public schooling
over abject poverty. Personally, I embraced the change.
I struggled with the hypocrisy and cliquishness I encountered in my small Christian school and relished
the opportunity for a fresh start.

However, the transition to a public school was a
culture shock. I knew no one, and no one knew me. I
was introduced to words and actions I had never experienced before. I spent that first year keeping a low
profile, trying to steer clear of the many fights I witnessed and resist the peer pressure to help my classmates cheat on assignments.

My one healthy lifeline to acceptance and friendship was sports. I excelled at the sports we played in PE, especially basketball and soccer. Gradually, I made a few basketball buddies, and we all tried out for the JV and freshman basketball teams. I played well in the tryouts, and I felt like I was one of the better players in the freshmen class. I was devastated when I didn't make the final cut. Some of the kids who made the team were players I crushed in PE every day. But their parents were in the Booster Club. It was easier for the coaches to cut a kid without connections like me.

I decided not to risk rejection in the spring. Instead of trying out for the high school soccer team, I played in the county's recreational league. I was the top player on my team—a big fish in a little pond. Everyone in the league knew my worth. It was a fun season, and we won the little plastic trophy given to league champions.

RECOGNIZING POTENTIAL

By my sophomore year, a full year of showing out in PE paid off, and I made the JV basketball team. Fresh off that success, I tried out for the varsity soccer team in the spring. Since official tryouts had already taken place by the time basketball season ended, I was given one practice to prove I was worthy of making the roster.

I made the most of that practice and played like a kid possessed. As I made one impressive play after another, the head coach kept looking at his assistants and shaking his head in disbelief. By the end of practice, he seemed both giddy over acquiring a new toy and outraged that he was just now finding out about me. "Where the hell were you last year?" he asked. I just mumbled something about not knowing how things worked, hoping he never found out I was MIA (Missing in Action) because I chose a recreational league over the real thing.

I can't help but see parallels between my high school sports experiences and the modern church. People attending church have tremendous potential yet have no idea how to get plugged into more meaningful ministry. They do not know how to answer the calling God has placed on their lives or how to use their spiritual gifts. They are using their gifts and abilities to impact earthly endeavors rather than eternal ones.

Meanwhile, churches are struggling to find solid volunteers and staff members. They feel Jesus' words in Matthew 9:37b. "The harvest is plentiful, but the laborers are few" (ESV). Churches want more help, but don't know how to find it. Few churches have healthy systems in place to identify, train, equip, and utilize the people in their circle of influence. The natural outcome of this reality is that leadership is spread too thin, most of the body remains spiritually immature, and the church's impact in God's Kingdom is minimized. The right people in the right positions could make all the difference.

PROTECTING AND EQUIPPING

The year before I joined the squad, our varsity soccer team failed to make the playoffs. The first year I played,

I started every game, and our team outpaced everyone's expectations, making it to the third round of the playoffs. I was merely a role player that year, but my presence helped shore up previous weaknesses. The following year, I was voted to the All-Region team, and we again made it to the third round of the playoffs.

My senior year, we became one of the top ranked teams in the state, largely due to some key additions. We added a key freshman who strengthened our midfield. Another player transferred in from Florida and became an instant starter. Best of all, we picked up a foreign exchange student from Spain who could score and assist goals as naturally as walking.

We cruised to the Upper State Championship where we faced a team we outclassed in every way—every legitimate way, at least. Once we went up 2-0 in the first half, the other team's play turned dirty. A violent collision left me with a dislocated right knee. An egregious high kick to the head of our star freshman forced him to exit with a concussion. A purposeful and malicious head-butt to our foreign exchange student's face knocked him out of the game with an orbital fracture.

Our team fought their hearts out the second half, holding onto that 2-0 lead with substitutes and JV players. I watched from the sideline as the other team scored their first goal with 15 minutes left in the game, rattling our young and tired team. They scored two more times in the next ten minutes and walked away with a 3-2 win.

After the game, angry parents swarmed the referees, asking why they didn't issue red cards for the ridiculous number of dirty plays our opponents committed. They responded sheepishly, "Well, we didn't want red cards to determine the outcome of the game." But their decision to do nothing as our opponent illegally took us out did exactly that—it determined the outcome of the game.

Church leaders are to protect and equip believers. Our enemy prowls around, seeking whom he can devour. He's taking out believers and potential believers left and right, and the church is swallowing its whistle like those referees. We are too afraid to step on toes, too afraid to confront, too afraid to attest to an unpopular truth, too uncaring to invite and challenge potential leaders, too comfortable to put in the work discipling, and too busy judging others and entering petty debates.

I am probably coming across as a little harsh, but I am passionate about this topic. The church was meant for so much more than what we see in most of America. In Matthew 16:18, Jesus said, "I will build my church, and the gates of hell shall not prevail against it" (ESV). On the firm foundation of Jesus Christ, no power in hell can withstand the church's advancement. We should be storming the gates of hell and setting the captives free through the power of the Holy Spirit working through the church.

LOSING PEOPLE

Rather than storming the gates, the church is in retreat mode. Churches all over America are shrinking. Fewer and fewer people identify as church-attenders and more and more are identifying as nonreligious. According to a 2019 Gallup Poll, church membership in America has decreased from 70% in 1999 to 50% in 2019. The number of those claiming to have no religious affiliation has increased from 8% to 19% over that same two-decade timeframe.

We are losing young people at a faster rate. Twenty-nine percent of millennials have no religious affiliation, and the ones holding onto faith aren't plugged in. Only 57% of millennials who claim faith attend any religious gathering.

Churches don't attract and engage younger generations. We have dropped the ball when it comes to mentoring or providing meaningful ministry opportunities. We are failing to help them identify their God-given gifts and purpose.

Those who stay aren't growing and maturing. Church should motivate us to love and do good (Hebrews 10:24-25) and equip one another to do God's work and build up the church (Ephesians 11:12). We can't motivate one another to love if we project a gossipy, judgmental spirit. We can't build up God's church if we don't invite, challenge, and train believers to do ministry work.

CHANGING HOW WE LOOK AT DISCIPLESHIP

We are missing the mark when it comes to discipleship. Throwing sermons, Sunday school classes and Bible studies at our congregations isn't working. Our discipleship plans need to model Jesus and the early church. Jesus' mountaintop sermons softened hearts, but that's not how He discipled His followers. His true disciples lived life with Him. They ate with Him and worked with Him—and did ministry by His side. He made time to answer their questions, and He corrected them when they were wrong. He challenged them to do more than they ever thought they could do.

The early church ate together and prayed together and shared their resources and spiritual gifts. And the church grew exponentially.

I love the home church movement, which is growing around the world. I don't think it's the only way to do church, and it's not without its weaknesses, but you can't hide in a home church. There's accountability in a home church. You create stronger bonds between your brothers and sisters in Christ as you share your lives. As long as a home church is launched by Christ-centered leadership and a growth-through-discipleship mentality, it can be a beautiful thing.

> 〉 〉 〉 〉 〉 〉 〉 〉 〉 〉

Our job is to build, restore, and make new through the name of Jesus.

I am not part of a home church. I work for a non-denominational church called Renovation Church in Simpsonville, SC. We're no mega-church, but we have well over a thousand people who regularly attend.

When we formed our church, our senior pastor, Jeremy Havlin, felt led to write this vision statement: "Building disciples to go make disciples."

I love our vision statement. It aligns perfectly with God's purpose for the church, and it cleverly fits with our name, Renovation. Our job is to build, restore, and make new through the name of Jesus. As the discipleship pastor, I was tasked with developing a game plan for fulfilling our vision statement.

I decided to start with what I knew and created several programs. We offered men's and women's Bible studies, a mentoring program that partnered mature believers with new or struggling believers, and weekly life groups.

But these programs failed to produce many fully formed followers of Christ. Instead of developing disciples, what we offered turned into a glorified game of whack-a-mole for sin problems and connection needs. Those who were hurting joined our mentoring program or signed up for free counseling. Those in Bible studies enjoyed learning something new and meeting new people, but the knowledge they gained was rarely applied or failed to stick. Our life groups showed the most promise, but without clear direction and training, they were only as strong as the group leader. Many of them gravitated towards becoming social clubs that supported one another but displayed little spiritual growth.

FINDING THE RIGHT DISCIPLESHIP PROCESS

We discovered a curriculum called *Rooted*. It's a 10-week discipleship curriculum that was developed in Africa and adopted by Mariners Church in Irvine, CA. Week 1 is an introduction and meet and greet. Week 2 tackles the question of who God is. Week 3 is about how to connect with God. Week 4 discusses why there is so much suffering in the world. Week 5 deals with spiritual strongholds. Weeks 6 and 7 focus on serving and embracing your spiritual gifts. Week 8 is on giving. Week 9 shows how to share your faith, and week 10 focuses on the purpose of church.

An information-based class would have been useless to us, but this curriculum was discussion and application based. Five days of brief homework and prayer time per week softened and prepared our hearts for the weekly group meetings. The discussions fostered growth, encouragement, and accountability. Then we took what we learned and applied it. We shared a prayer experience that lasted over an hour. We confessed strongholds, repented, and prayed for release. We actively sought community needs and served together in food pantries and facilities for the disabled.

The goal of this class was to establish healthy life rhythms—reading the Bible, praying, removing strongholds, sacrificial giving, serving, faith sharing and celebrating. We also wanted the individuals who entered this program to leave as a group who loved and supported one another, doing life together as brothers and sisters in Christ.

I can't tell you how much this discipleship process changed our church. By the time we concluded the 10 weeks with a celebration service, strangers had become friends and family and casual Christians had become devoted followers. Marriages were strengthened. Those watching from the sidelines got involved and started serving. Our giving numbers skyrocketed as people began tithing for the first time. Our church felt more mature and more unified than ever before.

The *Rooted* curriculum is not a magical cure. There are other excellent discipleship curriculums that might work just as well. Here are some reasons *Rooted* worked so effectively for us:

1. We had complete buy-in from top to bottom. Instead of the traditional sign-up sheets and online registration, as if *Rooted* was simply another event, we made it the class that mattered. We talked it up for six months—from the stage, in our emails and newsletters, and in our personal conversations. By the time we launched, we had created excitement and anticipation. And it was all we offered. We shut down all other Bible studies, life groups, and special events. We responded to every request to get more involved or get connected with the same response: Sign up for *Rooted*. Sometimes ministries compete with one another for resources and member participation. But for *Rooted*, we formed a unified front and implored everyone to join one of these discipleship groups. Well over half of our regularly attending adults accepted the invitation and completed the journey. Discipleship can't be one of many options; it has to be the priority.

2. We established a clear process for training and developing believers. Churches are notoriously bad about training leaders. If you show a little willingness to volunteer and a little potential to lead, we plug you in. We could not afford to do that with this program. So, our staff went through the *Rooted* process first. Next, our

potential discipleship group leaders worked through the *Rooted* process. We hosted an intensive two-hour training, walking them through how to lead each week. Once we launched the groups, we prayed for each group leader by name and followed up with each leader at least once a week.

Churches are fond of talking about "Next Steps", which usually consist of step 1-get saved, step 2-get baptized, step 3-join the church, and step 4-join a small group. If pushing people in this direction is the beginning and end of your church's discipleship process, it's unlikely that you will produce many disciples. Our church wasn't. By providing a clear direction for how we planned to build disciples and then equipping leaders to facilitate the process, we changed the culture at our church.

3. We provided common ground and a firm foundation. Most churches are made up of people from different religious experiences and backgrounds. Too often, churches assume people understand more than they do. The discipleship program helped us identify areas where people needed more information or assistance in understanding.

    Several members who had been Christians for years, even decades, shared they never understood who the Holy Spirit was or what purpose He served. Lifelong Christians had never been baptized. Many members had no familiarity with breaking the bonds of spiritual strongholds. Respected leaders admitted they struggled with tithing. Christ-like men and women came to see God in a different light and develop new life-changing habits.

Our church taught the importance of the Holy Spirit and baptism, but like many churches, we assumed most people knew what we were talking about, and we failed to provide an opportunity for back-and-forth discussion on the topics.

We need to expect more from ourselves and our churches.

This process put all of our participants on the same page, unifying us and creating a firm foundation. It's a starting point. Now we are working on the second level of discipleship training with five separate classes, one for each of the five disciplines we feel Christ fostered in His disciples. Bible study. Prayer. Worship. Evangelism. Leadership. These won't be lecture classes. They will be life application classes where we send people out to practice and live out the model Christ has provided in these areas.

We need to expect more from ourselves and our churches. No follower of Christ should rest until they have found someone or some church to disciple them, and no church should rest until they have an effective plan in place to disciple members. To be effective, a discipleship plan must involve actively living and serving with fellow believers and daily application of spiritual disciplines.

Most church attenders are immersed in the world. They are bombarded by worldly perspectives in what they watch, what they read, where they work, and who they hang out with. We break free from the world and grow in Christ when we change our habits. We must immerse ourselves in the Word, in prayer, in worship, and in Christ-centered community. True discipleship involves opening up our hearts, our homes, and our schedules to others. Unless we disciple our people with intentionality and love, the way Jesus did, we will always feel like something is missing. We are meant to be fully formed followers of Christ, and healthy discipleship is the way to get there.

SMALL GROUP DISCUSSION QUESTIONS

1. Have you ever served in any capacity for a church? If so, what kinds of positions? What led you to embrace each role? If not, what has held you back from serving?

2. Have you ever been part of an intentional discipleship process? If so, how effective was it? If not, what has stood between you and a discipleship process so far?

3. If you had to create a discipleship process from scratch, what would it look like? How would it work?

4. Do you have anyone actively mentoring you and helping you grow? If so, describe how it works for you? If not, ask God to fill that role in your life.

5. Are you mentoring someone? If so, how can you take your role to the next level? If not, prayerfully consider what steps you should take to prepare for such a role.

Chapter 8
Body Parts

Christians overlook the implications of being part of the body of Christ. Paul taught about the body in his first letter to the Corinthians in chapter 12. I strongly encourage you to put this book down and read that entire chapter before we go on. Here's a key portion of the chapter:

The human body has many parts, but the many parts make up one whole body. So it is with the body of Christ. Some of us are Jews, some are Gentiles, some are slaves, and some are free. But we have all been baptized into one body by one Spirit, and we all share the same Spirit.

Yes, the body has many different parts, not

just one part. If the foot says, "I am not a part of the body because I am not a hand," that does not make it any less a part of the body. And if the ear says, "I am not part of the body because I am not an eye," would that make it any less a part of the body? If the whole body were an eye, how would you hear? Or if your whole body were an ear, how would you smell anything?

But our bodies have many parts, and God has put each part just where he wants it. How strange a body would be if it had only one part! Yes, there are many parts, but only one body. The eye can never say to the hand, "I don't need you." The head can't say to the feet, "I don't need you" (1 Corinthians 12:12-21).

The church, the body of Christ, is designed with different parts to create one whole, healthy body. We should have body parts consisting of every race, every nationality, every age, every socioeconomic status, every skill set, and every spiritual gift. Such a church would be unstoppable. Unfortunately, most of our individual churches are missing body parts. We should be storming the gates of hell, but a body missing an eye, an ear, a leg, and several fingers is lucky to still be alive, let alone leading an offensive. A body missing body parts has no recourse other than retreat.

DISCARDED GIFTS

We've already discussed some primary reasons our churches plod along with missing appendages—blindness to potential, poor discipleship training, and complacency towards sin and accountability. Paul points out one more reason in the 1 Corinthians 12 passage. We are missing body parts because we don't value certain body parts. We've essentially cut them off ourselves.

Ephesians 4:11-13 says, "Now these are the gifts Christ gave to the church: the apostles, the prophets, the evangelists, and the pastors and teachers. Their responsibility is to equip God's people to do his work and build up the church, the body of Christ. This will continue until we all come to such unity in our faith and knowledge of God's Son that we will be mature in the Lord, measuring up to the full and complete standard of Christ."

These verses list five important gifts God gives the church—apostles, prophets, evangelists, pastors, and teachers. Notice how long these roles will continue to equip His church—until we are unified and mature in our faith and knowledge of Jesus and fully measure up to His perfection. Does this sound like any church you know? Have you ever been to a church where everyone in the church seemed to act just like Jesus? Yeah, me neither. I've only met a handful of people in my life who I would label as Christ-like, let alone a whole church or the big "C" church.

A straightforward reading of this passage seems to clarify that God is still providing these gifts, yet many denominations immediately dismiss the first two list-ed—apostles and prophets. According to these church-es, those gifts are dead. It's difficult to equip a church without two of the most important gifts.

MISUNDERSTANDINGS AND MISNOMERS

I believe the debate over whether we still have apostles is just a misunderstanding. Some people believe be-cause Paul and the 12 disciples were the only men spe-cifically referred to as apostles, only those specifically called into leadership by Jesus Christ Himself, in per-son, could be called apostles. No verse specifically con-firms this theory, and the passages in Ephesians 4 and 1 Corinthians 12 seem to refute the idea. The Greek word Paul uses in these passages, *apostolous,* is also used in 2 Corinthians 11:13 and Revelation 2:2 to describe false apostles. It's hard to believe that the early church had a serious problem with leaders pretending to be Pe-ter, Paul, or John. It's much more likely that Paul and John are using the term apostles to refer to a larger class of church leaders, men who formed and over-saw a group of believers. These false apostles weren't impersonating the 12 disciples; they were pretending to be leaders who were called by God when, in reality, they were servants of Satan who were promoting false teaching.

I believe the gift of apostleship Paul refers to is found in believers God has called to oversee ministries. They are the top leaders—the motivators and visionar-ies who start ministries and push them forward. Our Senior Pastor at Renovation Church, Jeremy Havlin, is someone who displays this gifting. We don't call him an apostle, but he demonstrates the spiritual attributes of apostleship.

God has called Pastor Jeremy to begin and grow ministries. He started a youth group from scratch and grew it to over a 100 kids. He started a missions organization in Nicaragua called One By One International, which focused on providing resources and services for underprivileged youth. A staff of three became fourteen. Hundreds of kids came to know Jesus and thousands received life changing care and counseling.

Pastor Jeremy's current mission is leading Renovation Church. We are less than six years old, but you would not know it from our size, resources, and impact. God deserves all the glory, and He could have brought Himself the same glory in a different way, but it is evident to me that our church's health is tied to Pastor Jeremy's God-given gift of apostleship.

I am convinced that most of the men we call Senior Pastor or Lead Pastor or Founding Pastor are actually apostles. Somewhere along the way we grew uncomfortable using the title "Apostle." Perhaps this is because some people who want to be called Apostle preach shaky theology or exhibit unhealthy power dynamics or maintain questionable financial systems.

Everyone seems to prefer the title "Pastor," but the title does not fit most lead pastors. The Greek word translated as pastor in Ephesians 4:11 is *poimen*. The literal definition of this word is "shepherd." A shepherd is supposed to care for the needs of his flock. Those that have this gift are likely to excel in hospital visitations, counseling, and grief care. Pastors are relational by nature and love working with people and meeting individual needs.

No offense to senior pastors, but that description doesn't seem to fit most top leaders. The lead pastors I've encountered are much more passionate about the big picture. They focus on presenting the Gospel in a new way, starting new ministries, sharing big ideas, and equipping leaders. They languish in pastoral roles like hospital visits, performing weddings and funerals, and counseling hurting people. They might perform these functions, and they might even excel at them, but it zaps their energy because they weren't designed for such roles. Apostles aren't shepherds.

Imagine what it would be like if we allowed our leaders to use their God given gift a majority of the time, rather than calling everyone a pastor and expecting them to be good at everything. Imagine if we let our apostles lead and provide the church with direction, and we let our teachers focus on teaching the Word, and we sent out our evangelists as preachers and missionaries to the unchurched, and we let true pastors watch over our care and counseling needs. Imagine how much healthier our churches would be.

HEARING FROM THE LORD

While the gift of apostles is often misnamed and misused, the gift of prophets has suffered a worse fate. Most churches have severed this body part and staunchly resist any attempt to reattach it.

The devil has done an amazing job to belittle and ostracize this gift. He has spread his lies effectively and planted many false prophets in the world to ensure that we distrust anyone who claims the gift of prophecy. We cannot afford to dismiss this gift because the devil has marred its name.

Prophecy shouldn't weird us out. Simply stated, prophecy is receiving a specific message from the Lord—a message you couldn't know without a revelation from God—and sharing the message with others. In my circle of experience, an audible message from God is rare. The message is usually downloaded directly into a believer's mind as a thought and sometimes delivered in dreams or visions.

We shouldn't hinder the gift of prophecy because we fear false prophets. God also gives the gift of discernment and a blueprint for identifying false prophets.

But if someone claims to be a prophet and does not acknowledge the truth about Jesus, that person is not from God (1 John 4:3).

The best litmus test for assessing a prophetic message is God's Word. The two should never disagree. The message should always bring glory to the name of Jesus Christ. If someone claiming to be an Apostle or Prophet adds or removes anything from Scripture with their messages, then run from that leader. The Apostle John reveals the heavy consequences of such teaching.

If anyone adds anything to what is written here, God will add to that person the plagues described in this book. And if anyone removes any of the words from this book of prophecy, God will remove that person's share in the tree of life and in the holy city that are described in this book. (Revelation 22:18b-19)

I realize some false teachers value prophecy and "new revelation" more than the Word of God. That theology is scary and dangerous. God gave us His Word to protect us, and the insights He gives us through the gift of prophecy will always be true, always agree with God's Word, and always bring glory to Jesus Christ. Since we have these safeguards to protect us, we can safely open our hearts to receive this gift.

I believe most, if not all believers, can experience this gift. A prophet is simply a believer who is especially gifted at hearing direct messages from God. We need prophets. Prophets warn us and encourage us. They help us walk the path God has for us when that path seems inexplicable from a human perspective.

EXAMPLES OF PROPHETIC GIFTS

We have prophets at our church. We don't call them by that name, and they would be terribly uncomfortable if we did, but that's the gift they have. One such lady is Ms. Rose. Over ten years ago, she received a vision during a prayer meeting. In the vision, she saw her church shrink to a handful of people. Then, suddenly, the church came back to life and every seat in the sanctuary was filled with people she didn't recognize. After the meeting, a friend of hers approached her and asked her if she had seen anything while praying. It turned out that her friend had seen the same vision. They felt sure this vision came from the Lord, but it didn't seem to make any sense. Her church, Westside Baptist, was healthy and strong, and a steep decline seemed unlikely.

Five years later, her vision was fulfilled. Her church of 600-700 people had dwindled to under 100. Sustaining the church building and staff salaries was no longer financially feasible, and they were facing closure. Our church, Renovation Church, was meeting in a movie theater. We had 600 people and several staff members, but we had no building and very few resources. Through some providential meetings and discussions, Westside Church invited us to take the reins of their church and form one united congregation. Everything about the merging process was a blessing to our church. Suddenly, our body of believers had a permanent home and access to ample resources. Best of all, the men and women from Westside that stayed with us provided us with incredible leadership and maturity. This partnership increased both our physical size and spiritual maturity. Our first service as one church fulfilled Ms. Rose's vision as we filled that sanctuary to capacity.

We also have an Elder with this gift. Recently, I asked the Elders to pray about me pursuing my doctorate degree. Our Senior Pastor loved the idea. Our Executive Pastor was on board. I was pretty sure it was going to be a slam dunk passing through our Elder

Board. The answer came back, "Yes, but not now." I was confused. I had more time on my hands than ever before due to the pandemic of 2020. We were just about to enter summer, my slowest season. I could not imagine a better time to start a load of doctorate classes. I asked why. It came down to the fact that one guy on the Elder Board, the one with the gift of prophecy, felt like the Lord said, "Yes, but not now." Once he spoke this feeling, the rest of the Elder Board confirmed it through prayer.

I wasn't upset, but this decision made no sense to me. I started imagining reasons the Lord might say "not now." Was my grandfather-in-law, who was in poor health, going to pass away? Was something going to happen to one of my kids? Would schools be shut down by COVID-19? What will happen for waiting to make sense?

Then, a week later, God downloaded a plan for a book into my mind. Every topic and chapter came to me instantaneously, and I fleshed out a complete outline within minutes. I had thought about writing a book before, but I had never written more than a few short stories and essays. I never seemed to have enough time to undergo such a project.

I could not shake the desire to write this book. The idea lit my heart on fire and consumed my mind. Just ask my beautiful, understanding, long-suffering wife. If I had loaded up on doctorate classes this summer as I had planned, I would have never written this book. It would have remained a pipe dream that would have likely died. If this book serves any real purpose for God's Kingdom, it will be because some godly men listened to the Holy Spirit's leading rather than what they could see and understand in their flesh.

My heart grieves at the thought of all the messages from God that have been hidden or rejected because we don't embrace this gift. Our churches are walking around with no ears because we've cut them off.

MISSING OUT ON OTHER GIFTS

Paul refers to several other spiritual gifts in his writings, with 1 Corinthians 12 and Romans 12 providing the two most comprehensive lists. None of his lists are quite the same which indicates to me he never intended to provide an exhaustive list. God passes out all kinds of spiritual gifts, and all of His gifts are good and valuable. He talks about the gift of faith, the gift of serving, the gift of giving, the gift of encouraging, the gift of leading, the gift of healing, the gift of performing miracles, and the gift of speaking in tongues.

These lists strike me as very matter-of-fact. For Paul, there was no debate about the validity of these gifts. He was more troubled by people striving after the more prestigious gifts rather than embracing their own. This is still a problem for the modern church. We honor and esteem the gift we call "Pastor" and the gift of teaching, but we rarely celebrate the other gifts, and outright reject some of them.

The gift on this list that causes the most controversy is speaking in tongues. I will readily admit that in my youth, I was one of the first people in line to throw a stone at those churches who allowed speaking in tongues. I thought they were a bunch of lunatics.

The mental picture in my mind whenever the topic came up was of people running up and down aisles or convulsing on the floor while yelling gibberish. Once again, Satan influenced some churches to do it the wrong way to deter good churches from wanting to do it the right way. Crazy video clips of Charismatics Gone Wild played in my mind and hardened my heart to the possibility of praying in the Spirit.

Fortunately, some godly men and women I highly respected helped soften my heart. Seeing the gift of tongues used properly, coupled with some sound teaching on the topic, convinced me that this is a gift that is both available and useful. If you are skeptical about speaking in tongues, I encourage you to read 1 Corinthians 14 carefully. I can't think of a good reason why Paul, inspired by the Holy Spirit, would spend an entire chapter explaining the significance of speaking in tongues and how it should be used in our churches, if it was a gift that was no longer accessible to the church. If every tongues-speaking church actually followed Paul's instructions on speaking in tongues, the devil probably wouldn't have been able to get away with making us fear this gift.

Many churches have shackled their prayer ministries. When you speak in tongues or pray in the spirit, as Paul also puts it, the words coming out of your mouth are not your own; they are the Holy Spirit's. I think it's safe to say that the Holy Spirit knows what to say and prays much better than I do, and His words have considerably more power. Just think how much more effective the prayers of our people would be if we let the Holy Spirit give us the right words. It's a shame we shy away from this gift.

MISSING OUT ON MIRACLES

Perhaps the most troubling gift kicked to the curb is the gift of miracles. It's amazing how we can quote Jesus when He says, "I tell you the truth, anyone who believes in me will do the same works I have done, and even greater works, because I am going to be with the Father" (John 14:12), and deny the existence of miracles and healings in today's Church. Jesus' teachings can be enigmatic, but His message here is straightforward and uncomplicated. If we believe, we can do what He did. We have the power of God living inside us, and the power of God seated next to the Father of Heaven, constantly interceding on our behalf.

This truth is also beautifully illustrated by Paul.

I also pray that you will understand the incredible greatness of God's power for us who believe him. This is the same power that raised Christ from the dead and seated him in the place of honor at God's right hand in the heavenly realms. Now he is far above any ruler or authority or power or leader or anything else—not only in this world but also in the world to come. God has put all things under the authority of Christ and has made him head over all things for the benefit of the church. And the church is his body; it is made full and complete by Christ, who fills all things everywhere with himself (Ephesians 1:19-22).

We have the power that raised Christ from the dead inside us, yet we don't believe we can perform miracles. Everything has been placed under the authority of Christ for the benefit of the church, and we believe God is withholding miraculous healings and prophetic words from His Bride, the Church.

> > > > > > > > > >

We have the power that raised Christ from the dead inside us, yet we don't believe we can perform miracles.

I would have to write a series of books to describe all the miracles we've seen at Renovation Church. Miracles of provision and blessing and restoration and healing. Our assistant worship leader's twin brother was diagnosed with a brain tumor. Judging by the PET scans and MRI, the doctor said he was 99% sure it was a glioblastoma, an extremely aggressive and deadly brain tumor. Without surgery, he would be dead in weeks. Surgery would buy him a year or two. His family was devastated, shell-shocked that their 55-year-old brother, father, and friend could be taken so early and so quickly. The surgery was scheduled as soon as possible. On the day of the surgery, the family gathered together for moral support while the church prayed for a miracle. When the surgeon walked out to share the result of the operation, he looked perplexed. He revealed the tumor wasn't a glioblastoma. It wasn't even malignant. It was a benign tumor that was easily removed in its entirety. He saw no reason to believe that there would be any lasting effects. The man was healed.

There are two types of people who listen to true stories like this. Those who believe God miraculously answered prayer, and those who think the doctor badly misdiagnosed the brain tumor. Those who have faith God still works miracles, and those who don't. Those who do, see miracles in many places. Those who don't, wouldn't see a miracle even if they witnessed a body come back from the dead. The Pharisees refusing to accept Lazarus's resurrection is one example that comes to mind.

I choose faith.

I tell you the truth, if you had faith even as small as a mustard seed, you could say to this mountain, "Move from here to there," and it would move. Nothing would be impossible (Matthew 17:20).

I believe seeds for every gift are planted inside our churches. We water those seeds with truth and watch them grow. If we embrace, nurture, and utilize all the spiritual gifts God provides, we will become the whole, healthy body of Christ Jesus intended us to be. Then, the gates of hell wouldn't stand a chance.

SMALL GROUP DISCUSSION QUESTIONS

1. In the churches you've attended, which spiritual gifts have been honored the most? Which spiritual gifts have been neglected or rejected?

2. Why do you think miracles and faith healings and prophetic messages are so rare in today's church?

3. Have you ever witnessed or known someone who experienced one of these gifts? If so, share the experience with the group.

4. Do you know what spiritual gifts God has given you? (There are spiritual gift tests online if you need help).

5. How are you using your spiritual gifts?

6. How could you use your gifts to make an even greater impact for God's Kingdom?

Chapter 9
Unity

What Martin Luther accomplished to bring about the Reformation of the Church might be the most important ministry work done since the first century. Luther certainly had his flaws, but what God did through the courage and obedience of one man is nothing short of astounding. The Roman Catholic Church was the most powerful entity in the entire world. Its leadership steered the Church so far off course that the Word of God was nearly unrecognizable. Martin Luther stood up to the church when doing so usually meant death. He led the charge in removing several ungodly practices in the church and once again made the truth of Scripture the focal point of the Church. By elevating the Word of God back to its rightful position and making Scripture and sound teaching available to the masses, Martin Luther became the catalyst for one of the biggest revivals in history.

Once Luther proved that church leaders could be in error and undermined the authority of the Roman Catholic Church, it was only natural that others would follow his lead. Over the next few hundred years, one man after another took issue with a doctrine or tradition in their church and left the church to form a new denomination.

There's no telling how many denominations we have today. I tried to research the topic, but it's a quagmire. Some articles report as few as a couple of hundred, if you lump them together in broader categories. If you don't use broad strokes, the number of denominations reaches the tens of thousands. Just look at the Baptist denomination: American Baptists, Central Baptists, Conservative Baptists, Free Will Baptists, Fundamental Baptists, Independent Baptists, National Baptists, Primitive Baptists, Progressive Baptists, Reformed Baptists, Separate Baptists, Seventh Day Baptists, Southern Baptists, and United Baptists. You would think that I just gave you a fairly exhaustive list of Baptists, but this list is a small sampling. And you would experience entirely different styles of service procedures, worship music and preaching depending on which Baptist door you walked through.

Being part of a denomination has its benefits. Denominational ties can help with organization and streamlining resources and provide accountability and oversight. The main denominational players have been responsible for countless church plants, hospitals, universities, and mission organizations.

So, I will not tell you that denominations are of the devil ... but they sure have been used by the devil.

WALLS AND DIVISIONS

Fights between denominations and within denominations have left the Church fractured and disconnected. Instead of building up one another, the enemy has convinced us to build up walls between us and our fellow brothers and sisters in Christ. The spirit that permeates these fights is one of pride. We carry with us a self-righteous, holier-than-thou mentality. We nitpick one another's flaws and hurl insults at each other. We refuse to work with one another and question each other's salvation.

It's especially hard to justify all the divisions in the church when we read Paul's words to the church in Corinth.

I appeal to you, dear brothers and sisters, by the authority of our Lord Jesus Christ, to live in harmony with each other. Let there be no divisions in the church. Rather, be of one mind, united in thought and purpose
(1 Corinthians 1:10).

The Corinthian church's division was caused by members in the church touting their favorite human leader, either Paul, Apollos, or Peter. The same mindset that led to our denominational splits. We championed a human leader over Christ's command to pursue harmony and unity.

DANGEROUS TONGUES

Once we allowed so many divisions to take place, we cemented those divisions with our tongues. We used our words to tear down those who disagreed with us.

We must be extremely careful with our words. Proverbs tells us that "death and life are in the power of the tongue" (18:21a ESV). Our words can breathe life into a person or ministry, or our words can suck life out of a person or ministry.

We are commanded to use our words to build up.

Don't use foul or abusive language. Let everything you say be good and helpful, so that your words will be an encouragement to those who hear them (Ephesians 4:29).

James provides us with the bluntest assessment of the power and danger contained within our tongues.

And among all the body parts, the tongue is a flame of fire. It is a whole world of wickedness, corrupting your entire body. It can set your whole life on fire, for it is set on fire by hell itself. People can tame all kinds of animals,

*birds, reptiles, and fish, but no one can tame
the tongue. It is restless and evil, full of deadly
poison. Sometimes it praises our Lord and
Father, and sometimes it curses those who
have been made in the image of God. And so
blessing and cursing come pouring out of the
same mouth. Surely, my brothers and sisters,
this is not right!* (James 3:6-10).

No, it's not right, and we will not escape the consequences of the bitter seeds we plant in our heart when we tear down others. Our words defile us. Jesus explained this to His disciples in Matthew 15.

*Hear and understand: it is not what goes into
the mouth that defiles a person, but what
comes out of the mouth; this defiles a person*
(Matthew 15:10-11 ESV).

Jesus shared these words after being attacked by the Pharisees for not upholding their man-made traditions. They bashed Him over religious procedures, and He warned them that their words were defiling their hearts. This revelation should make us sit up and pay attention.

WARPED PERSPECTIVES

Once seeds of pride and jealousy and bitterness are planted in our hearts, our perception will become skewed. To give you an idea of just how warped our viewpoint can become, I must admit that I grew up thinking that Billy Graham was a bad guy. Yes, you read that correctly. Billy. Freaking. Graham. In my circle of influence, his name would spawn derision and dismissal. Most of you probably think that putting down Billy Graham is like putting down Mother Teresa. Well, I hate to break it to you, but these early mentors of mine had a problem with Mother Teresa, too. She was tied to the Catholic Church, which equated with the devil's workshop.

Why Billy Graham? I never got a clear explanation, but the overall impression I got was that it had to do with him watering down the Gospel and forming friendships with obvious sinners. A friend of sinners ... I seem to recall someone else being accused of that in the Bible. I think it was Graham's willingness to befriend and counsel both conservative and liberal Presidents that pushed my ultraconservative bubble over the edge—even though God used Paul to do much the same thing the last few years of Paul's life. Paul spent time with, and swapped friendly banter with, several ungodly Roman leaders while in Rome. Who better to share the Gospel with than a ruler who had the power to make changes throughout the entire land?

As an adult, I looked into Billy Graham's life for myself and shook off my previous misperception. I recently read one of his biographies. Billy Graham is an incredible example of how much God can do through a believer who is singularly focused on using his or her spiritual gift to impact God's Kingdom. This man left an incredible legacy, one where millions of people came to know Jesus through his ministry. Yet, even he could not escape the vitriolic attacks of his brothers and sisters in Christ.

ATTACKING OUR OWN

I think the church has come a long way in the past decade. I believe we are far less judgmental and much more open to working with one another than we were before, but we still have a long, long way to go. We are still cannibalizing some of our best.

In early 2020, Francis Chan sent shock waves through the Evangelical world by sharing how God used him in a remote village in Myanmar to perform miraculous healings. In one instance, he laid hands on and prayed over a little girl and her brother, both of whom were born deaf, and after he prayed, they could hear for the first time.

The surprise for me about this story was finding out that this event was the first time Francis Chan had played a part in such a healing. With the faith he demonstrates, and the power of his teaching, and the way he seems to live his life, I assumed God had already used him to heal someone at some point. That's the respect and admiration I have for the guy.

For some Evangelicals, these miraculous claims prove Francis Chan is a fraud and a charlatan. They were already suspicious because Chan had spoken at a conference alongside some charismatic prosperity gospel preachers. He even acted cordially in their presence, shaking their hands and posing for a picture with them.

I read articles calling Francis Chan a heretic and a false teacher. All because he believes in modern miracles and has shown a willingness to interact with religious leaders who hold different viewpoints.

It is well known that Jesus associated with notorious sinners—zealots and prostitutes and tax collectors. Jesus also ate with Pharisees. He met with them publicly and privately, shared meals with them, and discussed Scripture with them. The Pharisees were way off base in their teaching, and they were keeping people from experiencing a closer relationship with God, yet Jesus still extended love and relationship to those willing to accept it.

What better way to change the culture of a church than to change the heart of its leaders? How are we supposed to help our brothers and sisters who are in error, doctrinally, see their mistake if we refuse to have anything to do with them? Harsh words on the page of an editorial or blog are unlikely to have any positive effect. People are more effectively swayed relationally. If we listen, we will gain a better understanding of what to say, and if we show love, we improve our chances of persuasion.

WHO ARE WE TO JUDGE?

We are so quick to judge others, to put them down and cut them off from fellowship, but the Bible says to do the opposite, and it says so over and over again.

*Don't speak evil against each other, dear
brothers and sisters. If you criticize and
judge each other, then you are criticizing and
judging God's law. But your job is to obey the
law, not to judge whether it applies to you. God
alone, who gave the law, is the Judge. He alone
has the power to save or to destroy. So what
right do you have to judge your neighbor?*
(James 4:11-12).

*So why do you condemn another believer?
Why do you look down on another believer?
Remember, we will all stand before the
judgment seat of God. For the Scriptures say,
"As surely as I live," says the Lord, "every
knee will bend to me, and every tongue will
declare allegiance to God." Yes, each of us will
give a personal account to God. So let's stop
condemning each other. Decide instead to live
in such a way that you will not cause another
believer to stumble and fall* (Romans 14:10-13).

Reading these passages, and the many others like them, should make us exceedingly cautious about condemning our fellow believers' flaws. Holding firm to the truth of the Gospel is important. We must speak out and condemn false teachings and false teachers. Embracing sin and false teaching in the church is just as dangerous as withholding grace and love. Leaning in either direction is going to end in misery for a church.

But consider the possibility that maybe we've given up on certain people within our churches, and certain people within other denominations, a little too soon. And, maybe, just maybe, some of the fights we've engaged in and divisions we've caused weren't necessary or healthy.

Not believing Jesus is the Son of God is a deal breaker. Whether sprinkling a baby has any merit, is not. That we are saved through a belief in the saving power of Jesus' death and resurrection is a fact worth fighting for. Where you stand on the five points of Calvinism is not.

HANDLING DISAGREEMENTS

Striving for truth and a better understanding of God and His Word is something we should all strive for, but Paul makes it clear in 2 Timothy 23-26 how we should handle disagreements on nonessential points.

Again I say, don't get involved in foolish, ignorant arguments that only start fights. A servant of the Lord must not quarrel but must be kind to everyone, be able to teach, and be patient with difficult people. Gently instruct those who oppose the truth. Perhaps God will change those people's hearts, and they will learn the truth. Then they will come to their senses and escape from the devil's trap. For they have been held captive by him to do whatever he wants (2 Timothy 23-26).

The church must stop the self-mutilation and start embracing the spirit of unity. We need all of our body parts connected and growing stronger through grace and love. I am convinced that the reason the Church isn't advancing in America is because our spiritual gifts are scattered across disconnected, individual churches.

The church must stop the self-mutilation and start embracing the spirit of unity.

Some churches attract great teachers but lack the faith to see God move. Other churches hear God's voice and feel His presence but struggle to maintain sound teaching. Some churches excel at serving and community outreach but struggle financially for the lack of good stewardship. Imagine what would happen if the church became unified and shored up one another's weaknesses, forming a united front, healthy and whole.

REAPING THE REWARDS OF LOVE AND UNITY

Renovation Church has experienced firsthand the beauty and impact of a church community that works together and loves one another despite denominational and racial differences.

When we launched Renovation Church, we had a body of believers committed to the cause ... and that's about it. We had no money, no resources, and no building. Our first meeting was held at a charismatic church called Bridgeway Church. Not only did they graciously let us use their facility while we worked out a plan to meet in a movie theater, but they also processed all of our tithes, for free, as we waited for our nonprofit paperwork to be approved. Without their help, we would have been stuck.

Once we moved into the theater, we could not afford all the sound equipment we needed. That's when Simpsonville First Baptist, perhaps the largest and most prestigious church in our town, loaned us two complete sets of speaker equipment free of charge. They even let us borrow a trailer to load the equipment in and out of the theater each Sunday.

For the first couple of months, our headquarters was an upstairs room in our youth pastor's house. We had nowhere to set up office space or meet with people during the week, as we were a mobile church that loaded into a theater every Sunday morning and had to be out by noon the same day. That is when Bethlehem Baptist Church, one of the largest African American churches in our community, invited us to rent space from them. They had recently closed their private school, so they had an unused wing available during the week. We could not have afforded to rent space at their normal rental fees. So, they offered us a rental agreement that was one-fourth of their normal asking price. Why would a predominantly African American church invite a brand new, predominantly white church to work alongside them in their beautiful home for a fraction of normal income? I cannot think of any reason other than the love of Christ. They were obeying Jesus' command to love one another.

So now I am giving you a new commandment:
Love each other. Just as I have loved you,
you should love each other. Your love for one
another will prove to the world that you are
my disciples (John 13:34-35).

This is how we convince the world to embrace the truth about Jesus Christ—through our love for one another. Instead of a reputation of divisiveness and hypocrisy, the Church should be known for being full of peace and love. If our churches were full of people who displayed the overwhelming peace that comes from knowing God and the overflowing love that springs from understanding Jesus' love for us, then people would flock to our churches. Who wouldn't want unity, peace, and love in their life? If we live how Jesus commands, that's what we find.

Because our church has been blessed through other churches, building up and loving other churches has been hard-wired into our DNA. We have made it our mission to knock down barriers between churches and share love and resources.

CHURCH COOPERATIVES

Humanly speaking, our senior pastor, Jeremy Havlin, and our worship pastor, Joe Cuyar, deserve most of the credit for all the initiatives we've undertaken to work with and help other churches. They are constantly networking with other church bodies. Pastor Jeremy is part of at least three different Senior Pastor groups who support one another and share ideas. Joe seems to know at least half of the worship leaders in the southeast. Together, they came up with our Church Cooperative and Worship Cooperative initiatives.

For Church Cooperative, we invite church staffs from all over the community to share a meal with us, worship with us, and swap stories, ideas, and resources with one another. At one table you will see senior pastors laughing and swapping stories. At another table, you will see youth pastors discussing ways to engage their youth. Another table will be full of connection pastors sharing ideas and resources they've used to retain people and get them plugged in. Then, off to the side is a whole table of worship pastors talking about the latest in fashionable haircuts and skinny jeans. Just kidding. I'm sure they are having deep, meaningful discussions about worship and their sense of style just comes naturally.

We have so much to learn from one another, and it's encouraging to know we aren't in this spiritual struggle alone. How great would it be if churches with an abundance of resources shared their resources with struggling churches? I'm not just talking about money. Financial resources would be a small part of the equation. Just as valuable are resources such as time, facilities, people, spiritual gifts, training manuals, and ministry expertise. How great would it be if churches that excelled in a particular area provided free training to help other churches excel in the same area?

Sharing is what we have tried to provide with Worship Cooperative. Every semester, we open our doors on Monday nights for free equipping classes to people interested in leading or serving in worship related ministries. We provide classes on every aspect of leading worship, whether its vocal training, music theory, instrument lessons, or AV training. Class members not only receive instruction, but they get to experience lifelike practice and hands-on training. Several churches send us their people so they can hone their craft and better lead worship in their home churches.

People have asked us why we offer this service for free. It's because we love the church, and we are all united under Christ. Ultimately, it all belongs to God, and when you embrace that truth, it's much easier to let go of what appears to be yours. In a little under six years of existence, we have given well over $50,000 to local churches in love offerings. We have loaned out entire worship teams on Sunday mornings to serve and lead worship in other churches. We have given more than $500,000 to missions organizations that we have no control over. You would think this kind of generosity would make our finances tight, but it is impossible to out-give God. Jesus tells us in Luke 6:38, "Give, and you will receive. Your gift will return to you in full-pressed down, shaken together to make room for more, running over, and poured into your lap. The amount you give will determine the amount you get back." We have experienced this promise. The more we've given, the more we've been blessed.

WORKING TOGETHER

We believe God is doing something special in our community. Churches seem to be more open to working together, despite their differences, than ever before.

Baptist, Presbyterian, Lutheran, Charismatic, Methodist, Nondenominational, Black, White, Hispanic—all coming together for a time of prayer, worship, or community impact.

I think churches fear that they will wander from the truth if they work alongside churches with different viewpoints. Our experience working with other churches has shown the opposite to be true. By working together and sharing our ideas and experiences, churches gravitate back toward biblical truth. Charismatic churches consider a more structured approach to using their gifts. Fundamental Pastors open their hearts to gifts they thought were long dead. Churches with no racial diversity hold hands and pray with people of another color. We all have blind spots, and when you work together with a bunch of godly men and women who have access to both the Bible and the Holy Spirit, you are much more likely to realize your blind spots.

We are better together. I know it's a strange supporting argument for unity, but consider the Tower of Babel in Genesis 11. God told Noah and his children to spread out over the earth and fill it. Mankind didn't listen. Instead, they formed a huge community in the land of Babylonia. In their ambition and pride, they decide to build a tower all the way to heaven. Knowing what we know today about science and the universe, I think it would have been hard for me to take this plan seriously, but God took it seriously. He understood the implications of mankind having the capability to build skyscrapers some 4,000 years ago.

In Genesis 11:6 God says, "The people are united,

and they all speak the same language. After this, nothing they set out to do will be impossible for them!" That comment has always stood out to me. It's a remarkable statement. When people are unified, they can accomplish anything they put their mind to. And, without access to the Holy Spirit, God knew that mankind would set its collective mind on pursuing evil in every way imaginable. When He confused our languages and separated us, mankind's progress was delayed long enough for Jesus to come at just the right time and atone for our sins—granting us access to the Holy Spirit and His power to overcome sin.

If a godless people with a unified spirit and purpose had this much potential, imagine the potential of a unified church, *with* the power of the Holy Spirit. The devil wouldn't stand a chance.

We may look different, talk different, think different, and worship different, but we have a great unifier in Jesus Christ. He is the Cornerstone that can crush all petty differences. If we can agree on who Jesus is, then we have a bond through Jesus Christ that makes us brothers and sisters.

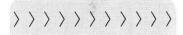

He is the Cornerstone that can crush all petty differences.

Jesus' final prayer with his disciples, before his death, was one for unity.

I pray that they will all be one, just as you and I are one—as you are in me, Father, and I am in you. And may they be in us so that the world will believe you sent me (John 17:21).

If we remain in Jesus, we will be unified. If we are unified, the world will believe that Jesus is the Son of God.

SMALL GROUP DISCUSSION QUESTIONS

1. What are your church denominational experiences? What were the pros and cons of being a part of each denomination you've experienced?

2. What are the topics that seem to cause the most division within the Church?

3. What are the beliefs and practices you think are definitely worth fighting for?

4. On a scale from 1-10 where 1 = no problem and 10 = serious problem, where would you rank the dangerousness of your tongue? If you don't mind sharing, share one example when your tongue got you in big trouble, and one example when your tongue encouraged someone.

5. What practical steps can we take to control our tongues?

6. What practical steps can we take to mend and overcome divisions in the Church?

Chapter 10
Love

Teachers are notorious for complaining about students in faculty lounges. I tried to steer clear of such conversations when I taught middle school and high school English, but I can recall getting sucked into at least one. There was a girl who I will refer to as Meg who had us pulling out our hair in frustration. After a solid first semester, Meg stopped trying. She turned in tests and quizzes blank. She slept through class. She snapped at teachers who corrected her behavior. Most alarming of all, she flirted with male peers, teachers, and administrators in highly inappropriate ways.

We had no idea what to do with Meg. So, we vented. In the middle of swapping stories of her outlandish behavior, Meg's guidance counselor, Lydia, walked in. I don't know if you have ever met someone who made you think, *this is what Jesus must have been like,* but that was Lydia. She couldn't make the blind see or the lame walk, but she could mend a broken heart or fragile psyche through sheer love and empathy.

Lydia didn't scold us. Her words and body language communicated that she understood our frustration, but what she shared shut our mouths. Eyes welling with tears, Lydia described Meg's home life.

Meg's family lived in a rundown trailer in a sketchy trailer park. Her mother was addicted to meth and often incapacitated. Meg was forced to become her younger siblings' primary caretaker. She was the one who got up in the middle of the night to feed and change her infant sister. She cooked the meals for the family—at least when there was food in the house. Near the end of each month, when the welfare check was used up, Meg stashed uneaten food from the school cafeteria in her jacket pockets to provide for her siblings. The mother had a boyfriend, also an addict, who recently moved into the home. Lydia had good reason to believe this boyfriend was sexually abusing Meg, but she could not convince Meg to report him for fear of having social services break apart her family.

"If you really want to help Meg, I encourage you to do a home visit. Experience for yourself what she faces every day."

Meg's teachers took Lydia's advice. We got her address from the attendance office, picked a day, and drove to her trailer park unannounced. The driveways were unpaved. The trailer had broken windows and holes in the siding. Meg was the one who greeted us at the door when we knocked. When she saw who was at the door, a jumble of emotions flashed across her face. Shock. Joy. Worry. Pride from meriting a home visit from her teachers, but anxiousness about what we would think.

My first impression of the inside was the smell. Some mixture of body odor, feces, cigarette smoke and meth vapor. It took willpower to keep my hands from shooting up to my mouth and nose to block the stench. The living room was dark, but it was hard to miss the naked baby sitting on a piece of cardboard in the middle of the floor. They had run out of diapers, and the cardboard play area was their solution. Once my eyes fully adjusted to the dark, I was able to locate the mother on a couch, stoned out of her mind. Behind her, standing in the corner, was her boyfriend. As soon as we introduced ourselves, the boyfriend slunk out of the home, not to be seen again during the visit.

We didn't stay long, maybe thirty minutes. The mother was largely incoherent, and we had all the information we needed at that point. Our frustration with Meg had completely dissolved, replaced by compassion. We were highly motivated to help this poor young girl and her family.

We stockpiled food and diapers for the family and bought the children several new outfits. Extra counseling sessions were worked into Meg's school schedule, along with afterschool tutoring in each subject area. After the home visit, Meg started accepting my open invitation to get picked up for church. Her siblings came, too. I made sure they always went home with a large Hot 'N Ready pizza from Little Caesar's.

The effect of these changes should surprise no one. Meg's grades improved. So did her attitude and peer relationships. With a little love and support, she became a new person.

SEEING PEOPLE AS GOD SEES THEM

People don't often equate God's omniscience with His love, but the two are connected. We find it difficult to love sinful people because we don't understand them. But God does. He is aware of our genetic flaws. He notes our dysfunctional environments. He witnesses every abusive word or action that shapes us. He is with us for every tragic outcome. He sees the spiritual attacks others can't.

When God commands us not to judge others it's not just because we have no right to as sinners. His command is also a protection for us because we are not equipped to accurately judge others. Our perspective is grossly limited and tainted by sin.

〉〉〉〉〉〉〉〉〉〉

Choosing to love rather than judge protects us and leads us to godly outcomes.

So God has removed the burden of judging others and replaced it with a command to love. We are to love others as we love ourselves and put their needs ahead of our own. We are to love everyone, from our closest friends and family to our worst enemies. Choosing to love rather than judge protects us and leads us to godly outcomes. I thank God someone with a Christ-like mindset encouraged Meg's teachers to give her the benefit of the doubt. We were ready to write her off. After the home visit, Meg's behavior made perfect sense. There were legitimate reasons why she was sleeping in class, snapping at teachers, and acting inappropriately. Understanding her situation opened our eyes to Meg's potential once her physical and emotional needs were met. Meg was an entirely different student once she experienced our love and support.

I am convinced we can see such radical turn-arounds in our churches, too. With the right kind of love and support, church members can reveal their untapped potential.

Nothing is more important than how we love God and our fellow brothers and sisters in Christ.

Most important of all, continue to show deep love for each other, for love covers a multitude of sins (1 Peter 4:8).

Our love can overcome past sin and point people to Jesus. Jesus' love can change anyone. The key is love.

Personal and spiritual growth comes from embracing God's love and seeing ourselves through His eyes. There's nothing special about us outside of Christ, but who we are in Christ should fill us with strength and confidence. We are children of the King of Kings and Lord of Lords!

*For all who are led by the Spirit of God are
children of God. So you have not received a
spirit that makes you fearful slaves. Instead,
you received God's Spirit when he adopted you
as his own children. Now we call him, "Abba,
Father." For his Spirit joins with our spirit to
affirm that we are God's children. And since
we are his children, we are his heirs. In fact,
together with Christ we are heirs of God's
glory* (Romans 8:14-17a).

Think about the implications of this truth. The One
who created everything calls us His children. We are
the adopted children of the King of the Universe. That
makes us princes and princesses. Our prospects and
potential are limitless because we are heirs to the
Kingdom of God.

When we are wallowing in guilt and shame, we
should remind ourselves that God has already paid for
our sins. When we accept Jesus' love and sacrifice for
us, all of our sins, past, present, and future, are wiped
from the record books. No barrier exists between us
and God. So much so that God refers to His followers
as priests.

*But you are a chosen race, a royal priesthood,
a holy nation, a people for his own possession,
that you may proclaim the excellencies of him
who called you out of the darkness into his
marvelous light* (1 Peter 2:9 ESV).

Before Jesus died on the cross, only the high priest was allowed to enter the Holy of Holies and approach God. When Jesus breathed His last breath on the cross, the veil that formed a barrier between God and His people was torn from top to bottom. This was a sign for us that Jesus' death made it possible for any man or woman to approach God and enjoy a relationship with Him.

From that moment on, everyone who accepts Jesus as their savior becomes a priest, a chosen minister for doing God's work in meeting spiritual needs. We are not second-class citizens of heaven. We are God's own sons and daughters who have been chosen to form a royal priesthood. We are all worthy of great ministry, not because of our own skills and pedigrees, but because God lives inside us and works through us because He loves us.

CHANGED BY LOVE

When we realize the extent of God's love for us, it should change us and motivate us to share God's love with others. One of my favorite examples of the transformative power of God's love is a friend of mine named Wayne.

When I first met Wayne, he had one of the worst cases of foot-in-mouth disease I had ever encountered. He simply could not control his tongue and spoke his mind, no matter what the topic or situation. There were occasions where I had to step in and put out fires Wayne started with offensive or ill-advised comments.

Strangely, Wayne has the gift of encouragement.

He has a great big heart and goes out of his way to build others up, but he couldn't seem to resist alienating people with his sometimes harsh and sometimes questionable perspectives.

I'm sure there were several factors involved, but when I think about how different Wayne is today than he was when I first met him, I recognize two factors. First, he met Lisa. Lisa is smart, capable and reserved. She has the gift of discernment. When Wayne and Lisa fell in love, Wayne's gift of encouragement made Lisa feel special and boosted her confidence. Lisa's gift of discernment and quiet strength kept Wayne in check. The love they developed brought healing to the deep wounds of previous marriages. They are much stronger believers together than apart.

The other aspect that changed Wayne was his prayer life. One day he asked me what I thought about praying in tongues. He told me he thought it was a load of crap and probably demonic. I told him that while it was often misused, I believed in the gift of praying in tongues. I had never prayed in tongues. The roots of my fundamental upbringing still strangle that gift. But I told Wayne that he should read 1 Corinthians 12-14 and watch a sermon series by Robert Morris called "Free Indeed" and consider the possibility that praying in tongues is biblical.

The next week, Wayne came back all excited and told me he had been praying in tongues all week, and the experience was revolutionizing his prayer life. Wayne has become an incredible prayer warrior. When he prays, miracles happen. Don't bring your prayer requests to Wayne unless you are sure you want them answered. He spends at least an hour every morning praying and singing praises to God. Wayne understands God's love for him and is grateful for all the blessings God has given him. In response to God's love, Wayne is vocal about his love for God. He is constantly praising God, posting about God and singing about God. God's love has changed Wayne, and Wayne's love for God has changed his family.

CHANGED BY ADOPTION

Not long after Wayne and Lisa married, they decided to adopt a child. Most parents want to adopt children as young as possible, but Wayne and Lisa adopted a demographic that is rarely adopted, a high school student. They adopted a fifteen-year-old named Sierra.

Sierra's childhood was marked by poverty, neglect, and dysfunction. She was placed in foster care several times as her mother struggled with substance abuse. There were days when Sierra would go without food because they had no money and her mother was too strung out to do anything about it. To make money, her mother forced her to sell drugs off and on through elementary school and middle school. Sierra was bullied at school over her appearance and struggled with serious bouts of depression. Sierra was finally removed from her home for good after her mother tried to kill herself with a bottle of pills right in front of Sierra. Once she was back in the system, Sierra's low self-esteem and depression reached a critical point, and she spent time in a mental hospital in order to avoid harming herself. It was out of this situation that Wayne and Lisa adopted Sierra.

When they brought her home, Wayne and Lisa poured their love and attention into Sierra. For the first time, Sierra felt safe and secure. She had never attended church, but at her new parents' prodding, she attended our youth group where she was also loved and accepted. A few months into attending our youth group, Sierra gave her heart to Jesus. A few months after that, Sierra agreed to share her testimony with her youth group. She shared intimate details of her broken, poverty-stricken life before Christ and what it felt like to be adopted by Wayne and Lisa, and then to be adopted by her Heavenly Father. There were very few dry eyes in the student service that night, and several students gave their lives to Christ.

Such is the power of love. Three broken homes—Wayne's broken by divorce, Lisa's broken by divorce, and Sierra's broken by substance abuse—healed by love and blended together to form one beautiful, whole family. Sierra had been painfully shy and insecure, and her future seemed hopeless. Now she is a strong, confident young woman who has just joined the Army and is training to be a Chaplain's Assistant. Her future is bright.

God's love should give us the confidence and the strength to love others well. When we love others well, they are more likely to open their hearts to the truth of the Gospel. When they accept Jesus' love, they will turn around and share their faith and love with others. This is the cycle we should be perpetuating.

1 Peter 4:8 says, "Most important of all, continue to show deep love for each other, for love covers a multitude of sins." Wayne's family is a perfect representation

of how love can overcome all kinds of obstacles and right all kinds of wrongs. I wish our churches looked like Wayne's family. Wayne is White—his email handle used to be HonkyTonkWayne, which fits his physical description. He has three Chinese daughters from a previous relationship. Lisa and her biological son are Puerto Rican. Sierra is African American. They are an amazing testimony of how love can overcome every difference and unite us into one family.

THE LOVE OF THE FATHER

Division and brokenness fill our world. Everywhere you look there is anger, bitterness, fear, and anxiety. More than ever, the church must lead with love. We must love one another well and love the world well. At the heart of it all, we must be motivated by Christ's love.

I want to conclude this book with a reminder of the kind of father God revealed Himself to be in the parable of the Prodigal Son. We find the story in Luke 15. The father in the story represents God. The younger son, who wants his father's money, but not the relationship, represents everyone who wants to live for himself rather than God. The older son represents all those who serve God out of a sense of duty rather than love.

Everything about this story oozes love. It was incredibly thoughtless and offensive for this son to ask for his inheritance before his father's death. Yet, the father said yes. Granting this request was an extraordinary act of humility. He sacrificed his personal wealth and status by giving away a large portion of his wealth to a son who wanted nothing to do with him. Refusing his son's request would have only led to bitterness and resentment, so with love, he allowed his son to make mistakes and learn the consequences of sin.

Love led the father to keep watch for his son's return. Love motivated the father to run to his son the moment he came into view. When the son tried to assume the role of a servant because of his sins, the father ignored his son's words. Instead, he called for the best robe in the house and put a ring on his finger, letting the whole world know he was the cherished son of his wealthy father. Then, they threw a big party.

This is the type of heavenly Father we have. He is the Father who will leave the 99 sheep who are safe and rescue the one who is in trouble. He is the Father who will toss a room inside out and upside down to find His missing treasure (Luke 15:3-10). He is the Father who will take us back and elevate our status to the highest rank the moment we humble ourselves and seek His voice.

You are not worthless. The gifts and abilities God has blessed you with are not second rate. God has a plan and a purpose for each of His children, and His Church works best when all of His followers are playing their part. If we block out the lies of this world and hold tight to the truths found in Scripture, we will recognize God's calling on our lives. Like children who love and trust their father, we will obey Him and allow Him to mold and shape us.

We can accomplish anything when God is working in us and through us. He is a good Father who loves you and wants to partner with you to impact His Kingdom. I hope you will embrace His incomparable love and let Him use you in great and mighty ways.

SMALL GROUP DISCUSSION QUESTIONS

1. Who are the people in your life that have believed in your ability to do great things? How have they shaped your life?

2. How does it make you feel to think of yourself as a child of God, a prince or princess, or a priest or priestess?

3. What is the most radical change you've seen in someone who has embraced the love of God?

4. How can we further embrace the love of God?

5. How can we further extend the love of God to others?

6. What will you do to increase your impact for God's Kingdom?

〉〉〉*ACKNOWLEDGMENTS*〉〉〉〉〉

Thank you to my friends and family whose love and support made this book possible. The following people deserve special thanks for helping me see this project through and offering their expertise:

Jeremy Havlin. You believed in my call to write before I took it seriously, and you supported it every step of the way.

Dean Coursen. You gave me the time and space to write, and your calm support gave me the peace of mind to move forward with confidence.

Clay Keller. No one was a bigger help in making my book stronger. Your editing advice and theological assessments were instrumental in shaping this book.

Karen Porter. Your professional editing advice was excellent and took my book to another level.

Amanda Thompson. Your love and support through all the ups and downs of getting this book to print meant the world to me. You are a gift from God.

ABOUT JASON THOMPSON

 **Jason Thompson** is a teacher, pastor, and author living in Simpsonville, SC. As a sports lover he spent most of his youth playing soccer, baseball, basketball, and sand volleyball. He graduated from North Greenville University on a soccer scholarship and received a Master's Degree in Teaching from Converse College. Before being called into full-time ministry as a pastor, Jason was a National Board Certified English teacher.

In 2011, Jason left the public school system to teach his favorite subject—the Bible. He has been a Teaching and Discipleship Pastor ever since, currently working at Renovation Church in Simpsonville, SC. He spends most of his working hours developing curriculum, teaching, and overseeing small groups and discipleship programs.

Jason uses both the Bible and his own personal experiences to motivate others to step into the role God designed them to fill. As one who experienced the pain of divorce and the redemption only God can provide, Jason is passionate about helping others see their potential in God's Kingdom.

Jason's greatest joy these days is spending time with his family. He is happily married to a beautiful and godly woman named Amanda. In addition to raising two boys of their own, Jason and Amanda are foster parents who feel called to provide a home for other children in need of stability and love.

If you would like to contact Jason or find out more about his ministry work, you can connect with him through his website worthnoless.com.

>>> *NOTES* >>>>>>>>>>>>>>>>>>>>>>>>>

Chapter 2

1. Jones, Sarah Bruyn. "72% Say Church Is Full of Hypocrites." Tuscaloosa News, Tuscaloosa News, 19 Jan. 2008, www.tuscaloosanews.com/article/DA/20080119/News/606100924/TL.

2. Banks, Adelle M. "Study Views Christians as Judgmental." Oklahoman.com, Oklahoman, 27 Oct. 2007, oklahoman.com/article/3157477/study-views-christians-as-judgmental.

Chapter 3

1. The illustration of punching people to demonstrate the consequences of sin is a variation of a sermon illustration I heard from Robert Morris of Gateway Church. Gatewaypeople.com.

Chapter 4

1. Kyle's nonprofit, Next Steps Today, is a great resource for battling drug addictions. This nonprofit is also a ministry well worth your donations. For more details, check out Nextstepstoday.com.

2. If you are looking for a ministry to support, I cannot think of a better option than House of Hope. Quite literally, they are pulling women and children out of a life of prostitution and equipping them with the Holy Spirit and an alternative means to make a living. For more details, check out Houseofhopeinternational.com.

Chapter 5

1. "Dwight L. Moody Quotations: Page 2 at QuoteTab." QuoteTab, www.quotetab.com/quotes/by-dwight-l-moody/2.

Chapter 7

1. Jones, Jeffrey M. "U.S. Church Membership Down Sharply in Past Two Decades." Gallup.com, Gallup, 8 Apr. 2020, news.gallup.com/poll/248837/church-membership-down-sharply-past-two-decades.aspx.

2. You can find everything you need to know about the *Rooted* Curriculum and resources at experiencerooted.com.

Chapter 8

1. For more details on the ministry work accomplished by One by One International, visit obointernational.com.

Chapter 9

1. Metaxas, Eric. *Martin Luther: The Man Who Rediscovered God and Changed the World.* Penguin Books, 2018.

2. "List of Baptist Denominations." Wikipedia, Wikimedia Foundation, 13 May 2020, en.wikipedia.org/wiki/List_of_Baptist_denominations.

3. Whalin, Terry. *Billy Graham: A Biography of America's Greatest Evangelist.* Morgan James Publishing, 2015.

4. Klett, Leah MarieAnn. "Francis Chan Says He Healed Deaf Boy, Girl in Rural Myanmar Village: 'My Faith Was at Another Level.'" The Christian Post, 12 Feb. 2020, www.christianpost.com/news/francis-chan-says-he-healed-deaf-boy-girl-in-rural-myanmar-village-my-faith-was-at-

another-level.html.

Chapter 10

1. Morris, Robert. "Set Free!" Set Free! | Gateway Church, 29 Dec. 2013, gatewaypeople.com/series/free-indeed?sermon=set-free.

Made in the USA
Columbia, SC
04 November 2021